Edward: The Uncrowned King

Christopher Hibbert

Edward: The Uncrowned King

Christopher Hibbert

St. Martin's Press · New York

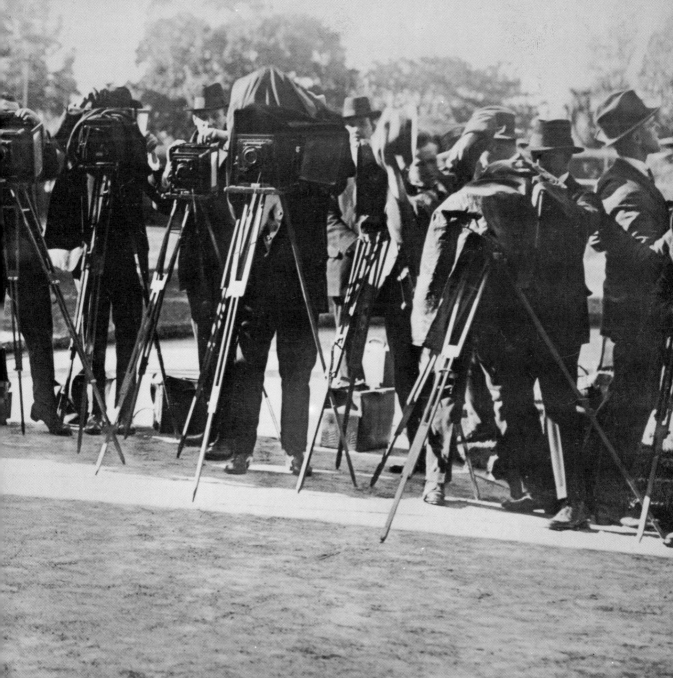

Frontispiece picture *shows a diffident Prince of
Wales facing a battery of cameras on his Australian
visit in 1920*

St. Martin's Press
175 Fifth Avenue
New York, N.Y. 10010

Contents

Introduction: 'Poor David'

He usually looked sad as a child. It was as though he were already aware, so one of his father's friends thought, that the future would weigh heavily upon him. Yet he was not really unhappy then. In later years he recalled delightful days at Windsor, riding in the Great Park, going for trips on the Thames in a big electric launch, pedalling his bicycle around the paths at Frogmore, past the urns and the rhododendrons and the mausoleum where his great-grandmother, Queen Victoria, lay buried with Prince Albert. Sometimes he would go up to the Castle and play hide and seek amongst the marble busts in George IV's Grand Corridor, or push his brothers about on the tall, wheeled ladders in the Library, or climb up on to the roof and explore the great expanses of lead, the valleys and ridges and chimney-stacks, all the more pleasurable to him 'because it was forbidden ground'. Most exciting of all were those occasional days when he went to visit his grandparents, King Edward VII and Queen Alexandra, who seemed to him to be 'bathed in perpetual sunlight', and who provided him with a glimpse of a world far different from the one he knew, a much more thrilling and exotic world, mysterious and remote, in which life was lived in an intriguing atmosphere of brandy fumes, cigar smoke and scent.

He adored his grandfather who, though surrounded by amusing, rich and raffish friends, always found time to talk to him and to laugh with him. He was not in the least nervous with him as he was with so many other older people. When he saw him at Sandringham he rushed up to him to kiss his hand and, on being picked up, to kiss his cheek. On opening the door to an unexpected visitor there, he had been heard to call out carelessly, 'Come in, there's nobody here, nobody that matters, only Grandpa.' He had once even been known to interrupt the King's conversation at table. He was reprimanded, of course, and sat in silence until given permission to speak. 'It's too late now, Grandpa,' he said. 'It was a caterpillar on your lettuce but you've eaten it.' With his father he was never on such terms.

When he was born in June 1894 at White Lodge, Richmond Park, his father recorded his unaffected pleasure in his diary. For the Duke of York, the future King George V, was by nature an affectionate, deeply domestic man who loved babies and delighted in the prospect of a close and happy family life which they seemed to promise him. Yet he conceived it his duty, as his children grew up, to compel them to share his own rigidly held concepts as to form and behaviour and the demanding obligations of their birth. Lord Derby once claimed to have suggested to him that he was unnecessarily strict with his children, an unwelcome criticism which apparently elicited the reply, 'My father was frightened of his mother; I was frightened of my father; and I am damned well going to see to it that my children are frightened of me.' The accuracy of George V's description

1 The christening, 1894. A Queen and three Kings

of his father's attitude to Queen Victoria and of his own feelings towards Edward VII may, perhaps, be doubted. It may also be doubted that his response to Lord Derby's strictures was a considered one, more likely it was provoked by anger, since he was notoriously averse to criticism. But whatever the conditions were in which the remark was made, there can be no doubt that, whether intentionally or not, he did succeed in making his sons frightened of him. He appeared to them as a stern intimidating figure with whom they were never completely at ease. In his less severe moments he addressed them in a bluff, insistently jovial manner which they found both irritating and embarrassing; and when he was angry with them he was terrifying. No words that his eldest son ever heard in later life were 'so disconcerting to the spirit' as the summons, usually delivered by a footman, that his father wanted to see him in the library.

Prince Edward – or David as he was always known in the family – 'often felt that despite his undoubted affection' for his children, his father really 'preferred children in the abstract, and that his notion of a small boy's place in a grown-up world was summed up in the phrase, "Children should be seen, not heard." It was once said of him that his naval training had caused him to look upon his own children much as he regarded noisy midshipmen when he was captain of a cruiser – as young nuisances in constant need of correction.'

Certainly his children were constantly corrected. They felt themselves to be permanently on parade in their father's presence. They had to have their stockings pulled up tight over their knees; their necks had to be encircled in starched Eton collars; the pockets of their sailor suits had to be sewn up so that they could not put their hands in them. A lanyard a fraction of an inch out of place or a sporran slightly awry would earn a parental reprimand of the utmost vehemence.

Nor was much comfort to be derived from their mother, who hated being pregnant and was disgusted rather than uplifted by the idea of giving birth. Queen Mary was kind enough to them; but there could never be any question of her taking their side against their father. 'I have always to remember', she used to say, 'that their father is also their King.' As her biographer has said of her, she 'never possessed the knack of winning the confidence of her sons in their boyhood.' Reserved and undemonstrative, she was as incapable of showing them a mother's affection as her husband was in communicating with them in any way at all.

In later life Prince Edward wistfully complained that he had never known the kind of loving sympathy that other children enjoyed. There had been servants who had seemed to love him, but he could never be sure whether or not this was because he would one day be their king. There was one servant in particular who was devoted to him; but in so unhealthy a way that the damage she did to his personality may well have been even more extensive than that caused by his feelings of isolation from his parents' sympathy and understanding. This was his nurse, an emotionally unstable woman who eventually, after three years' service during which she had never had even the briefest holiday, suffered a complete mental collapse. She virtually ignored Prince Edward's younger brother, feeding him so erratically that his stomach never fully recovered from the neglect; but

2 The child Edward with his parents, then Duke and Duchess of York

her devotion to Prince Edward himself was so obsessive that it drove her to pinching him and wrenching his arm when the time came for her to present him to his parents, in order that his tears and screams would lead to his being the sooner returned to her.

Denied any demonstrations of affection by his parents, Prince Edward was also denied any intellectual stimulus. His father took pride in his simplicity, his down-to-earth Englishness. He was slow, thorough, conscientious, conservative and tenacious – it was part of his strength as a king that he always remained so – but he had no intellectual curiosity, nor any taste for art. He read more than Edward VII had done, but as his second son's biographer has noticed, 'almost the only criticism of his father to be found in the length and breadth of his correspondence' is of an arbitrary decision to convert the bowling alley at Sandringham into a library. He preferred the life of a country squire to any other; and had always found it difficult to talk to many of his father's friends, particularly the beautiful and witty women and the foreign men, for he was conscious that his mind though shrewd enough was far from subtle. He did not altogether trust foreigners, anyway, and he detested travelling abroad. 'England is good enough for me,' he said. 'I like my own country best, climate or no, and I'm staying in it. . . . There's nothing of the cosmopolitan in me. I'm afraid I'm insular. . . . I'm not like my father.'

It was the tragedy of Prince Edward's young life that *he* was not like his father either, and that his father was determined to make him so.

If his father did little to encourage the development of Prince Edward's intellect and nothing to stimulate his interest in the arts, nor did his mother. For Queen Mary's own interest in art was prompted more by her passion for royal iconography than by admiration for the objects she collected as works of beauty in themselves. She was fundamentally a museum director *manquée*. 'I think I know something about arr-r-rangement,' her father-in-law used to say rolling his r's in his rather German way; and so did Queen Mary know something about arrangement. She was a good judge of furniture and china, and was a determined, not to say avaricious collector; but her reputation as an infallible connoisseur was certainly unjustified, and she never bought a notable picture. In any case, her interest in art did not develop until after Prince Edward had left home. While he was a child she appeared to be as little concerned with it as her husband was, and as vaguely suspicious as he was of artists and intellectuals of all kinds.

The limited outlook of his parents was shared, to a lesser extent, by his tutor, Henry Hansell, whose prowess as a sportsman seemed far more important to his father than any academic qualifications he may have possessed. Mr Hansell was, in fact, a totally inadequate tutor and well aware of his limitations. In his opinion it would have been far better had his charge been packed off to boarding-school; and this no doubt would, indeed, have proved the wiser course. Prince Edward would never have been a scholar, but he was an intelligent child capable of absorbing far more than the uninspired curriculum of his private schoolroom demanded. When he did come into contact with other boys he invariably found himself placed well towards the bottom of the class.

This contact with other boys outside his family took place for the first time when he was thirteen and was sent as a naval cadet to Osborne. King George V's third son, Henry, was

4

3 *The Royal Family at Osborne House, Cowes, in the summer of 1896. Prince Edward is third from left*

4 *Princess Mary (the Princess Royal), Edward, and Prince Albert of York (later George VI) in 1900. The following year Queen Victoria died and Edward's grandfather – Edward VII – came to the throne. The children were great favourites of Edward VII – the* two Edwards adored each other; they were often

sent to Eton; but clearly the King thought that his heir would be all the better for the more rigorous, more disciplined, less academic routine of a naval college. 'The Navy', the King said, 'will teach David all that he needs to know.' It was an unfortunate calculation.

After his training at Osborne the Prince went on to Dartmouth, completed the five years' course and passed his examinations. He was sent to sea for three months as junior midshipman aboard the coal-burning battleship, the *Hindustan*. He was worked very hard by the captain, a friend of his father, who expected him to 'know as much about a battleship in three months as it takes the average "snottie" three years to learn'. But he could not learn so fast; and, as he said himself, he would never have recommended anyone to sail in a ship under his command.

His naval training, such as it was, completed, Prince Edward was sent to France to improve his French. He stayed at the château of the Marquis de Breteuil, then travelled south to Arles, then on to Marseilles and Cannes and across the frontier into Italy, taking photographs wherever he went and revealing a more eager curiosity than he had ever shown at home. He obviously enjoyed this first taste of travel, and the relative freedom away from his father and the naval officers of Osborne and Dartmouth. Yet his shyness was now painful and acute; and although his smile was charming, it was as fleeting as it was rare. Photographers who caught him unaware showed the world how sad his face was in repose; and a picture of him painted in Paris by François Flameng, and reproduced by the London press, actually portrayed him wearing a worried frown.

He looked worried, too, so observers noticed, when, at the age of eighteen, he went unwillingly up to Oxford and entered Magdalen College as an undergraduate. He also looked absurdly young, as though he ought still to be at school; while his nervousness and tension, his lack of confidence were betrayed to everyone who stared at his short, slight figure in the streets and noticed the way he pulled at his tie, twisted his neck as a man will do when his collar is too tight, compulsively grasped his right wrist in his left hand – nervous and revealing mannerisms that remained with him for years. Yet during his two years at Oxford, he did seem to acquire more confidence. What he did not acquire was any aptitude for study. With varying degrees of interest and for varying periods – mostly short – he took up all kinds of sports and pastimes. He played tennis and golf; he went shooting and beagling; he hunted with the South Oxfordshire Hounds; he played soccer for the College's second eleven. He strummed on a banjo, and gave his fellow undergraduates at Magdalen further distress by practising the bagpipes in his room. But the sudden enthusiasms which these pursuits aroused were not matched by any devotion to learning. The President of the College pronounced an appropriate verdict when he said, 'Bookish he will never be.' He had never wanted to be so. He had been sent to Oxford against his own inclinations, and was deeply relieved when it was agreed that, having trained as a sailor, he should now have a taste of the Army by taking a commission in the Grenadier Guards.

Before joining the Army, however, he was sent abroad again, this time to Germany. During two visits, one in the spring, the other in the summer of 1913, he was as active with his camera as he had been in France. He stayed with his cousins, the King and Queen of Württemberg, at Stuttgart; and with the Grand Duke of Mecklenburg-Strelitz at Neus-

5 *In July 1911 Edward donned the Investiture robes as Prince of Wales*

trelitz; he went to Friedericshaven where he met Count Zeppelin; he took pictures of the stallholders in the market-place at Nürnberg and of the castles of Thüringia. He went shooting in the forests with various German relations; he went out driving with them in solid, gleaming motor-cars; he flew with them over the countryside which their ancestors had ruled for centuries. He had dinner with the Emperor in Berlin. He returned home with an affection for Germany which the coming war was not to break.

The Prince emerged from that war with his reputation enormously enhanced. Denied the opportunity of proving himself in battle, he had held staff appointments throughout; but countless stories had been told of his anxiety to get to the front, of his coolness under fire when he did get there, and of his compassion. Everyone had heard reports of his visit to a field hospital where arrangements had been made for him to see only the less severely wounded patients. He asked to see the others, and spoke to them, too. One hideously mutilated man, deaf, dumb and blind, was kept from him, however. He insisted on visiting him also; he knelt down beside him and kissed his cheek.

In the immediate post-war years the Prince's popularity continued to increase. Thousands of photographs appeared in the newspapers showing him on his travels round the world, conscientiously fulfilling his duties as his father's representative, diffident, charming, handsome, still looking like a boy.

His father, indeed, continued to treat him as a boy. He was obliged to acknowledge that his son was a highly effective, if often unpunctual, ambassador; but as the years passed and the Prince outgrew his immaturity the King displayed no wish to make use of his services in any other important capacity. On his return from his last official tour in 1925 he was thirty-one; but even so he was not allowed to undertake any duties more responsible than those expected of other members of his family. He was not actually forbidden to discuss affairs of state with his father's ministers, yet it was made plain to him that his father disapproved of his son doing so. The government papers that did find their way on to his desk were made available to him 'only with the greatest misgivings and after considerable resistance'. 'At the same time, in a manner never defined,' as he complained years later, 'I was expected to remain conversant with all that was going on in the world and to give the impression of being knowledgeable and well-informed.'

It was not only that his father considered him too flippant and pleasure-loving, too much given to unsuitable friendships and deleterious pastimes, too fond of informal, sloppy clothes, but also that his ideas and attitudes were far too modern, revolutionary even. His war experiences and his foreign travels had made him restless and impatient, eager for change, exasperated by the stuffy protocol and convention of the Court. He sincerely wanted to help ex-servicemen and the unemployed, the disillusioned young and the despairing destitute; and he wanted to do so in the informal, casual way that seemed so natural to him, yet so dangerous an innovation to his father.

After years of practice, he had become a competent public speaker; his excellent memory, particularly for faces, his easy conversational manner, and his intelligent questions all made it easy for him to make a success of his receptions of delegates and emissaries, his visits to institutions, the numerous ceremonies during which he was required to lay foundation

8

6 The Prince of Wales enters Magdalen College,
Oxford: October 1912

stones, cut tapes, walk round factories, declare shows open, present prizes, view exhibitions. But it was his social work which he himself considered far more important than his traditional, ceremonial duties; it was his obvious concern for the poor and the deprived which made him the most popular Prince of Wales that the country had known since the death of James I's son, Henry.

His social conscience had been awakened, it was said, on visiting a soup kitchen in a provincial town where he had seen a queue of silent, hungry men one of whom, much younger than himself, had no shirt under his coat. 'What can I do? What can be done?' he asked afterwards, pacing up and down anguished and depressed. It was a question he was to ask himself many times in the future as he walked through industrial towns with relentless energy, talking to workers and entering their houses. It was a question which he was never able to answer.

Frustrated in his efforts to play a more important role in governing the country, and in helping its less fortunate inhabitants, the Prince spent an increasing amount of time in trying to prove his worth in other ways. To his father's dismay – and in the face of much opposition – he took up flying; he persuaded his pilot to teach him how to fly the aeroplane himself; and one day, while the pilot watched with the utmost anxiety, he took up the aeroplane on his own. When he came down he behaved, so the pilot said, just like a schoolboy who had won a race.

He took up steeplechasing with even more enthusiasm. He was never a good rider; but he was an almost fanatically determined one, disregarding danger as recklessly as he did in the hunting field. To win a race, as once or twice he did, was exhilarating for him. It satisfied the latent desire in him to excel, to test himself 'against others on equal terms', as he put it, 'to show that, at least in matters where physical boldness and endurance counted,' he could hold his own. As with flying, however, steeplechasing was considered too dangerous a pursuit for a Prince of Wales; and in the way that he rode it probably was. He often fell off his horse with frightening force, and once was so badly concussed that he had to stay in bed for almost a month. After his father's severe illness in 1928 he was persuaded to give up steeplechasing for good. He took to golf and to gardening instead.

The gardening was done at a 'grace and favour' house, six miles from Windsor Castle, Fort Belvedere, 'a castled conglomeration', in the Prince's description, which, begun by William, Duke of Cumberland, had been enlarged by Wyatville on George IV's instructions. 'What could you possibly want that old place for?' the King had asked grumpily when his son had asked for it, 'Those damn week-ends, I suppose.' For the Prince's weekends, and the friends that came to spend them with him, had by now become yet another bone of contention between father and son.

The King's anxiety was understandable. Indeed, the older the Prince grew the more justified many of his father's strictures became. Of course, the King was often unreasonable. His own life was now regulated by rules more hidebound than ever. 'Everything had to be carried out according to precedent,' one of his servants recalled. 'Old forms and ceremonies that had been in use for centuries were scrupulously observed. The rules and conditions of service laid down for the Household in the reign of George III were still referred to when

10   7 *1914: Edward as a corporal in the O.T.C.*

Self.

any doubt arose, and "It has always been done that way" was considered the last word in any argument.'

George V had an almost morbid horror of change. He lived his life as though by clock-work, sitting down to his plain and quickly eaten meals at exactly the same time every day, going to bed every night at precisely ten minutes past eleven o'clock. The sight of anything new appalled him. 'What!' he once exclaimed in horror at the sight of an un-familiar object on the dinner table, an avocado pear which Prince Edward had ordered for him as a special treat. 'What in heaven's name is this?'

It was not surprising, then, that the Prince should be constantly criticized for having the wrong sort of friends and for wearing the wrong clothes, that an appearance at an official function without a top hat should call forth a visit from the King's Keeper of the Privy Purse and a stern warning that the Prince was becoming far too accessible, that he ought always to remember that the monarchy must 'retain an element of mystery, must remain on a pedestal'. Times were changing, the Prince protested.

Times, indeed, were changing; but the Prince himself was changing, too. Well aware of his popularity he was growing more and more vain about it; he was also growing more stubborn, more impatient of advice, more satisfied with his own judgement and opinions, and determined to have his own way. The King could not forbear from comparing the modest, quiet, domestic, dutiful behaviour of his second son, the Duke of York, with the far less praiseworthy conduct and attitude of 'poor David'.

The Prince enjoyed the company of his lively youngest brother, the Duke of Kent; but he had little in common with either the Duke of York or the Duke of Gloucester. He felt far more at home with the kind of fast, amusing, frivolous people who frequented the noisy night-clubs of the period, Ciro's, the Café de Paris and, his own favourite, the Embassy. In these clubs he could be seen dancing the Charleston in the early hours of the morning with an energy that seemed scarcely less than frenzied. His favourite partners were not the aristocratic débutantes of whom his father could have been expected to approve but actresses and divorcees and fashionable demi-reps.

During the war he had fallen in love with Lady Rosemary Leveson Gower, daughter of the Duke of Sutherland, who eventually married the Earl of Dudley's heir, Lord Ednam. Subsequently – and more deeply – he fell in love with Freda Dudley Ward, the estranged wife of a Liberal member of parliament and mother of two daughters of whom the Prince became extremely fond. Mrs Dudley Ward was an amusing, attractive young woman with a delightful voice and a disarmingly friendly, gregarious manner, 'tiny, squeaky, and wise and chic' in the words of Henry Channon, the rich, Chicago-born diarist and socialite. Lady Cynthia Asquith, who once saw her dancing with the Prince in the early days of their relationship, described her as 'a pretty little fluff with whom he is said to be rather in love. He is a dapper little fellow – too small – but really a pretty face. He looked as pleased as Punch and chatted away the whole time. I have never seen a man talk so fluently while dancing. He obviously means to have fun.'

The longer he knew Mrs Dudley Ward the more devoted to her he became. He went to see her as often as he could, and every day when he was in London. She returned his passionate love with a kind of tender, playful affection. When he was in one of his difficult, sulkily magisterial moods, she teased him out of it in the way that she might have overcome the pettishness of a spoilt child. It was generally agreed that she was very good *with* him and very good *for* him. It was also agreed that – as Sheridan said of George IV – he was 'too much every lady's man to be the man of any lady'. He had several other affairs, most notoriously with Gloria Vanderbilt's twin sister, Thelma, who had been married at the age of sixteen, divorced a few years later, and married for the second time to Lord Furness, the shipping magnate. She was an extremely attractive woman, and the Prince was immediately captivated. Soon he was almost constantly in her company; they were seen dancing together night after night, they went on safari together in Africa; on their return they were inseparable.

Yet the prince was growing rather tired of London social life, and the hectic pleasures of the Jazz Age. He now preferred the quieter enjoyments of Fort Belvedere, where in the early 1930s he could be seen in plus fours and rather garish sweater working in the garden, or, in the evenings, in Highland dress, marching round the dining-room table playing his bagpipes. He loved Fort Belvedere, his 'Get-Away-From-People-House' as he called it; and he was never so happy as he was when he could spend a week-end there with a few carefully chosen friends. 'I came to love it as I loved no other material thing,' he recorded. 'Perhaps because it was so much my own creation. More and more, it became for me a peaceful, almost an enchanted anchorage, where I found refuge from the cares and turmoil of my life.'

Indeed, so fond of Fort Belvedere did the Prince become that he appeared to resent the time that he was obliged to spend away from it. Now that his father was in failing health, he was at last given more responsibility; but he had found other more compelling interests by then and the new duties were not as welcome as once they might have been. He performed them adequately; but his relief to have them finished and to be back, happily occupied with the continuing improvements at Fort Belvedere, was obvious.

Never had he seemed so happy there as he was in the early weeks of 1934. Lady Furness was not with him, as she had gone on a visit to New York where she had aroused the interest of Aly Khan. But the Prince now had another, closer friend to whom Lady Furness had first introduced him three years before, Mrs Simpson. *1931*

Wallis Simpson came from an old American family in Baltimore. As a young woman she had married a pilot in the United States naval air service; and, after their divorce, she had found another husband more to her taste in the person of Ernest Simpson. Although he came from New York and had graduated at Harvard, Ernest Simpson looked like a very English gentleman, and always behaved like one. He had served in the Coldstream Guards and had become a naturalized British citizen. After his own divorce he had married Wallis in 1928 at Chelsea Register Office and had set up home with her in London.

Mrs Simpson was a smart, intelligent woman, good-natured but independent, determined, and outspoken. As she admitted herself she clung fiercely to her 'American ways and opinions – possibly to the point of exaggeration': her Baltimore accent was still very pronounced. The Prince, who was two years older than she was, found her entrancing.

She was not as good-looking as the other women with whom he had been in love, but her interests ranged wider; she was sympathetic and understanding, and, on occasions, very witty. The Prince felt he could talk to her about his work and the role he would soon be called upon to play; and, far from being bored, she encouraged him to do so. 'It all began', the Prince said afterwards, 'with something as simple as that.'

To some of those who met her for the first time the Prince's fascinated interest in her seemed rather strange, though, as Lady Diana Cooper said, she was 'admirably correct and chic'. 'She is a nice, quiet, well-bred mouse of a woman with large startled eyes and a huge mole,' commented Henry Channon, having been asked to lunch by Lady Cunard to meet her. 'I think she is surprised and rather conscience-stricken by her present position and the limelight which consequently falls upon her.' After a subsequent lunch party Channon decided, 'She is a jolly, plain, intelligent, quiet, unpretentious and unprepossessing little woman, but . . . she has already the air of a personage who walks into a room as though she almost expected to be curtsied to. At least, she wouldn't be too surprised. She has complete power over the Prince of Wales . . . . She has enormously improved him . . . . He is obviously madly infatuated and she . . . has completely subjugated him. Never has he been so in love. She is madly anxious to storm society, whilst she is still his favourite, so that when he leaves her (as he leaves everyone in time) she will be secure . . . . The romance surpasses all else in interest . . . .' As yet the general public knew little about it. Nothing had appeared in the newspapers; Mrs Simpson was discreet; Mr Simpson appeared complaisant; the King, of course, was not informed. A few days before the wedding of the Duke of Kent, Mrs Simpson was presented to His Majesty. It was the only time she ever spoke to him.

The King's life was drawing to its close. In 1935 he had reigned for twenty-five years and had become a well-loved institution. On his Jubilee Day that year the unmistakably enthusiastic acclamations had made him realize, as though for the first time, how really loved he and Queen Mary had become. 'I'd no idea they felt like that about me,' he said after a visit to the East End during which he had been cheered vociferously. 'I am beginning to think they must really like me for myself.' It was all very rum, he told the Archbishop of Canterbury, for he was 'a very ordinary fellow'. That was his triumph, of course. He *was* an ordinary fellow and yet he had been an exceptionally skilful king. There were few Englishmen who did not feel moved when he died.

He was buried in St George's Chapel, Windsor on 28 January 1936. His eldest son scattered earth over the coffin from a silver bowl and then came out into the cold, sunless air, his grey face sad and drawn.

He had lost little of his popularity with the public, though those who had had to work closely with him had noticed the gradual change in him of late. He was subject to moods of excessive irritability. His servants, to whom he had always behaved with extreme consideration in the past, began to find him thoughtless. For days on end he would not attempt to do any work before noon, and frequently men summoned for interview would be sent away without having seen him. It began to be whispered that his public duties were being performed in the intervals left in a life devoted to pleasure. Often excited, even exhilarated, he rarely seemed completely happy except when he was with Mrs Simpson. He was subject more and more to those periodic bouts of black depression to which he had been a victim for years and which drove him to mope in solitude.

For all this, he was still a much-liked figure of whom great hopes were entertained. As *The Times* commented, his many and varied attributes of experience and character 'could hardly fail to command the popular confidence and honest liking with which, in full store, he begins his reign.' It was widely expected to be a reign marked by change and experiment, an exciting reign in which cobwebs would be swept out of dark corners and reaction would give way to reform. It began well enough. On St David's Day, King Edward VIII made an effective broadcast in which he declared, 'I am better known to you as the Prince of Wales – as a man who, during the war and since, has had the opporunity of getting to know the people of nearly every country of the world under all conditions and circumstances. And, although I now speak to you as the King, I am still that same man who has that experience and whose constant effort it will be to promote the well-being of his fellow-men. . . .'

Soon afterwards, in July, while he was riding down Constitution Hill past crowds of cheering people after having presented colours to six battalions of the Guards, a man threw an object which looked like a bomb – but which turned out to be a loaded revolver – into the road in front of him. He reined in his horse, made some unconcerned remark, then, as *The Times* noted, 'calmly proceeded on his way'. The story of the King's coolness and composure was repeated all over the country to his increasing credit.

Yet the King was even more frustrated now than he had been as Prince of Wales. He had been keenly anticipating the authority and responsibility of kingship; but, as he soon found out, being a king was an 'occupation of considerable drudgery'. It was not altogether a discovery, since his father's conscientious attention to 'doing his boxes' had taught him what to expect. The 'interminable amount of desk work' with which he was immediately faced, nevertheless, came as something of a shock to him. It was 'all the more taxing for me,' he admitted, 'because if the truth must be known, I have never had much zest for paper work. Much more to my taste was what I called my "field work".'

It was all the more taxing, also, because he was finding it even more difficult to break with tradition than he had supposed it would be. He was able to do so at Fort Belvedere where he was his own master, of course. In February 1936, Lady Diana Cooper found 'the King unchanged in manners and love'. The 'glorious stationery' was new, but that was almost the only concession she found to her host's new status. Frock coats were still 'outmoded almost by law' and the servants were 'a bit hobbledehoy because HM wants to be free of comptrollers and equerries, so no one trains them'. As in the past, the King 'donned his wee bonnet' after dinner and marched round the table with his bagpipes, 'his stalwart piper behind him, playing "Over the Sea to Skye" and also a composition of his own'.

Away from Fort Belvedere, though, the King found life very tiresome. In his autobiography, as an instance of the resistance 'towards the most trifling change' that he encountered, he cited his quarrel with the Deputy Master of the Mint about which side of his face should appear on the new coins and stamps. He wanted the left-hand side of his face to appear as he thought that profile the better one; but the Mint insisted that the right-hand side must be shown, as it was a long-standing custom to reverse the profile of the sovereign with the advent of each new reign. King George V had looked to the left; so King Edward VIII must look to the right. The King was adamant. The Mint also stood firm. But in the end it was the King who had his way.

The background on the stamps was not changed, however; so that the King's head was turned away from the light, looking into the gloom. It was considered a significant portent. It was not the only one.

The King had insisted on watching the ceremony of his proclamation at St James's Palace. This was no serious break with tradition; but when the newsreel cameras moved from the trumpeters in the courtyard to the windows of the palace, their lenses caught a glimpse of Mrs Simpson standing next to the King. In July other revealing pictures appeared on the newsreels and in the press. The occasion was a palace garden party at which numerous débutantes were to be presented. He was clearly seen to be thoroughly impatient with the whole procedure, giving each girl a hurried nod, looking ineffably bored, and bringing the ceremony to an end when it began to rain. It had 'always seemed' to him that women were 'prone to attach an excessive importance to these affairs'. Since all the cards had been taken up, he had 'no doubt as to the social status of those débutantes who had been left, so to speak, at the far end of the carpet'; and he confessed himself 'at a loss to understand' that 'some parents' should have felt that 'without the Sovereign's personal bow of recognition, the presentation was not quite genuine'.

It was felt that here again the King had behaved tactlessly. Far better, it was suggested, to have abandoned the outmoded ceremony altogether than to have conducted it with such apparent boredom and perfunctoriness.

It was a small affair, though symptomatic of the King's growing thoughtlessness and mounting impatience which led him, for instance, to make drastic economies in the royal estates without seeming aware of the hardship caused to many employees who had long been in the service of the Crown. Those who knew him best had no doubt wherein lay the King's torment. At a dinner party at Windsor Castle at the end of March, the King, clinging to his 'secret and private life with a kind of desperation', so Lady Hardinge recorded, had spoken at length about George IV and Mrs Fitzherbert.

The trouble was that it could not remain a 'secret and private life' much longer, and that the King was fully determined to bring the issue to a crisis. In July he gave a dinner party at York House to which the Duke and Duchess of York and several members of the government were invited. Mrs Simpson was also there. Mr Simpson was not. Later on that summer the King went on a cruise down the Dalmatian coast aboard a luxury yacht, the *Nahlin*. Again Mrs Simpson was of the party, and many photographs were taken of her in the King's company. On his return he went to Balmoral where Mrs Simpson, who had stayed behind in Paris for a day or two, was later to join him. He was photographed meeting her at the railway station on the day that he had been asked to open a hospital extension in Aberdeen having delegated the duty to the Duke of York on the grounds that he himself was still in mourning.

Up till now, overt references to the King and Mrs Simpson had been successfully kept out of the British press. The temptation to publish reports and pictures of the *Nahlin* cruise

8 July 1917: the Prince of Wales with George V, examining a gas bomb at the Gas School at Helfaut, France

9 (Overleaf) During his voyage to India in 1922, Edward is met at Madras by the Viceroy, Lord Willingdon, and his wife. In the background is the Royal Indian Marine Steamship, 'Dufferin'

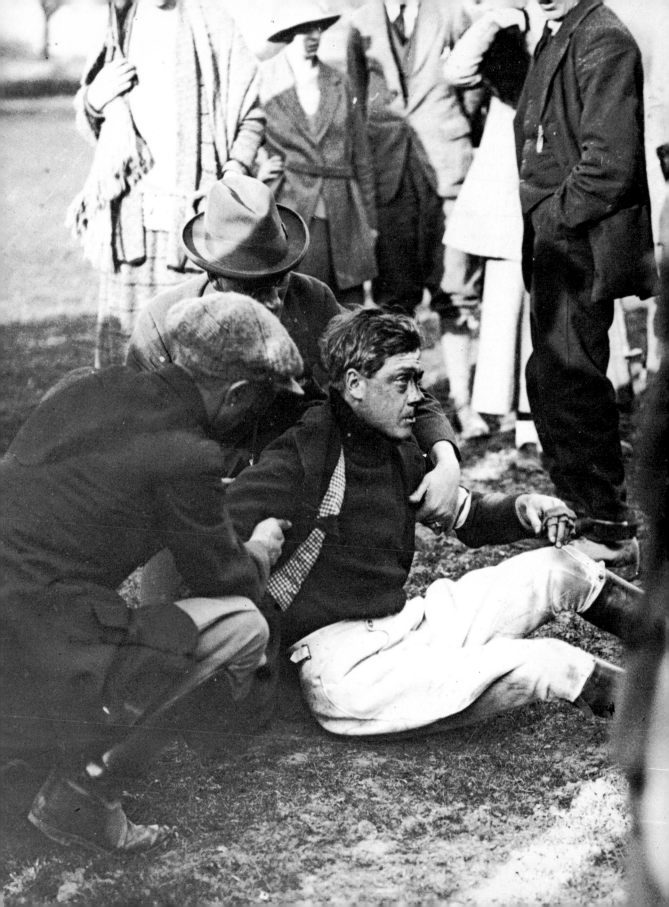

had obviously been insistent, but most editors had resisted it. There had been no question of *The Times,* under the editorship of Geoffrey Dawson, publishing anything yet; nor of the arch-conservative *Morning Post* doing so. The *Daily Telegraph* had even omitted Mrs Simpson's name from the list of the *Nahlin's* passengers; the *Daily Express* carried a photograph of the King in a dinghy from which his companion Mrs Simpson had been carefully excised.

The full picture of the two of them together in the dinghy was published in the magazine *Cavalcade,* while another similar picture appeared in the *Sketch* – to the consternation of Lord Camrose who immediately ordered that there should be no further references to the affair. But these were very rare indiscretions. Most newspapers subjected themselves to a rigid censorship. Even when Mrs Simpson was granted her divorce on 27 October, the peculiar significance of the case was not mentioned by those newspapers that referred to it at all. The King had taken precautions that this should be so. He had asked Lord Beaverbrook to go to see him, and had 'told him frankly of his problem'. 'My own desire', the King explained, 'was to protect Wallis from sensational publicity, at least in my own country. Max heard me out. "All these reasons," he said, "appear satisfactory to me – and I shall try to do what you ask." Without delay he began a prodigious task, unique in the annals of Fleet Street, where the mere suggestion of censorship offends. With the cooperation of Esmond Harmsworth [son of Lord Rothermere and chairman of the Newspaper Proprietors' Association] and several others, he achieved the miracle I desired – a 'gentleman's agreement' among newspaper editors to report the case without sensation. The British Press kept its words, and for that I shall always be grateful.'

No such control could be exercised over the American Press which for months had been printing all manner of news and conjecture about the affair. 'He will go nowhere without her,' the American public had been informed at the end of September. 'Hostesses who don't invite her don't get the King. In her company he never looks at another woman; he watches her all the time, fondly and intently.' On 17 October, the *Washington Post* said that he was determined to marry Mrs Simpson whatever the consequences; he had given his approval to the divorce suit; he might 'indeed have suggested it'. *Time* magazine ran story after illustrated story about the King's 'companion on numerous holiday excursions'. *Liberty* magazine published an article about 'The Yankee at King Edward's Court' and sold two and a half million copies of the issue in which it appeared.

Reading such reports, a British citizen living in America – or, as was afterwards suggested, one of its own correspondents – sent to *The Times* a long letter complaining of the 'dizzy Balkan comedy' which was being played out in London. Nothing would please the writer more, he said, than to hear that Edward VIII, who had proved himself 'an incalculable liability', had abdicated. 'The prevailing American opinion is that the foundations of the British throne are undermined, its moral authority, its honour and its dignity cast into the dustbin.'

Much impressed by this letter, Geoffrey Dawson had copies of it made and took one of them to Buckingham Palace where he asked the King's private secretary, Major Alexander Hardinge, to show it to his master. Hardinge told Dawson that the Prime Minister had

10 Concussion at Arborfield Cross point-to-point, 1924

already been to see the King to express his profound anxiety about the serious situation that was developing. The Abdication Crisis had begun.

Within six weeks it was all over. On 10 December the King announced his decision to abdicate. The next evening, after dining with his three brothers, his sister and his mother at Royal Lodge, he was driven to Windsor Castle to make his last broadcast to the nation.

'At long last I am able to say a few words of my own,' he began. 'I have never wanted to withhold anything, but until now it has not been constitutionally possible for me to speak. A few hours ago I discharged my last duties as King and Emperor, and now that I have been succeeded by my brother, the Duke of York, my first words must be to declare my allegiance to him. This I do with all my heart.

'You all know the reasons which have impelled me to renounce the throne. But I want you to understand that in making up my mind I did not forget the country or the Empire which as Prince of Wales, and lately as King, I have for twenty-five years tried to serve. But you must believe me when I tell you that I have found it impossible to carry the heavy burden of responsibility and to discharge my duties as King as I would wish to do without the help and support of the woman I love . . . .'

Although he sounded tired, it was a well-delivered speech, skilfully phrased and deeply moving. Many of those who listened to it were close to tears. The voice 'came out of the loudspeaker calmly, movingly,' Mrs Simpson recalled. 'I was lying on the sofa with my hands over my eyes, trying to hide my tears. After he finished, the others went away and left me alone.'

When the broadcast was over, the Duke of Windsor, as he now was, left immediately for Royal Lodge where his brothers were waiting to say good-bye to him. 'Dickie this is absolutely terrible,' the eldest of them had said earlier to Lord Louis Mountbatten. 'I never wanted this to happen; I'm quite unprepared for it. David has been trained for this all his life. I've never even seen a State Paper. I'm only a naval officer; it's the only thing I know about.'

But the naval officer had already become a king, and as the Duke of Windsor left Royal Lodge that night he bowed to him in the doorway; and their youngest brother, the Duke of Kent, 'watching, shook his head and cried almost fiercely, "It isn't possible! It isn't happening!"'

'But it had happened,' the Duke of Windsor commented. 'It was all over. . . . I was irretrievably on my own. The drawbridges were going up behind me. But of one thing I was certain: so far as I was concerned love had triumphed . . ."

The Duke and Duchess of Windsor were married at the Château de Candé near Tours, the home of a rich industrialist, Charles Bedaux. The Duke's friend, Major 'Fruity' Metcalfe, was best man; Mr Herman Rogers, at whose home in Cannes the Duchess had been staying, was also there. But no members of the royal family were present. Queen Mary noted in her diary: 'Alas! The wedding day in France of David.' After the ceremony had been performed according to French law, there was a subsequent marriage service by an Anglican clergyman who had volunteered to conduct it.

A honeymoon in Carinthia was followed by a trip to Germany. Hearing of his intention

11 In his album Edward captioned this portrait: 'Wallis [Mrs Simpson] was presented at Court at Buckingham Palace on 10th June, 1931'

to go to Germany, the British government became extremely worried about the effect that this would have on public opinion at home. There were rumours enough already in England that both the Duke and Duchess had strong Fascist sympathies; and these rumours had been fanned by reports that their wedding had taken place at the château of Charles Bedaux, who was a known Fascist sympathiser and was to commit suicide after the war rather than face the consequences of having been a collaborator. Lord Beaverbrook flew out to the Duke to try to persuade him not to go. But the Duke had lost none of his obstinacy. Protesting that he now had no official position, so was free to go where he pleased, he rejected Beaverbrook's pleas and went to Germany as he had planned to do. He was met by Dr Robert Ley, the alcoholic leader of the Labour Front, and was introduced to various other Nazi leaders, including Hitler himself. He did not much care for any of them; but photographs of him and the Duchess in their company were published all over the world, much to the satisfaction of Dr Goebbels.

While the war with Germany drew nearer, the Duke and Duchess moved about on the Continent from hotels to rented house, from Paris to Versailles and down to the Côte d'Azur. The Duke was happy; he loved the Duchess deeply; but he was restless. He would have liked to go home, to have a house in England, to have work to do, to play some part in helping his family with their official duties. He wrote to Neville Chamberlain, now Prime Minister, to offer his services; but the non-committal answer he received was, he knew, a polite refusal. He wrote also to his mother to ask her to set down her true feelings about him. Queen Mary replied, 'You will remember how miserable I was when you informed me of your intended marriage and abdication, and how I implored you not to do so for our sake and the sake of the country. You did not seem to take in any point of view but your own. . . . I do not think you have ever realized the shock which the attitude you took up caused your family and the whole nation. It seemed inconceivable to those who had made such sacrifices during the war that you, as their King, refused a lesser sacrifice. My feelings for you as your mother remain the same and our being parted, and the cause of it, grieve me beyond words. After all, all my life I have put my country before everything else, and I simply cannot change now.'

What distressed the Duke as much as anything else was that his mother wholeheartedly approved of the decision that the Duchess should not bear the title Her Royal Highness. 'Nothing in the aftermath of the abdication hurt [him] more than that gratuitous thrust. In his eyes it was an ultimate slur upon his wife, and, therefore upon himself.' Its effect, the Duchess complained, 'was to debar me in defiance of all custom from taking my place alongside my royal husband.' It was a slight which rankled with him for the rest of his life.

How strongly he felt about it was revealed in 1940 when once again he offered his services to the British government. He had come home to England from France the year before, and had been sent back to Paris as a major-general with the Military Mission to the French Command. On the fall of France he had fled to Spain and from there he had gone to Portugal. Churchill asked him to return to England. But, as he told his wife, 'I won't have them push me into a bottom drawer. It must be the two of us together – man and wife with the same position.' He was prepared to return on two conditions: he must be told

*12 The new King often found it difficult to veil his
dislike of ceremony: a garden party, July 1936*

beforehand what kind of appointment the government had in mind for him; and the Duchess must be accorded the same status as the other royal duchesses. The Duchess of Windsor had not been received at Court at all while they had been in England the year before; and the Duke was determined that this time he would force the hands of his family and the government and obtain the title and recognition for his wife that he felt so strongly was her due. The Duchess herself felt that this was scarcely the time to 'make an issue of so private a matter when the rest of Britain was fighting for its life.' And this view of the Duke's stipulations was naturally shared by those to whom they were addressed in London.

The government and the royal family were not to be coerced. The Duke could not come home on his terms. If he wanted to be of service, the Governorship of the Bahamas was vacant. He could go there, and was, in fact, desired to go immediately. After some delay, which caused a great deal of disquiet in London, the Duke accepted the appointment and sailed for Nassau.

The Duke and the Duchess arrived in the Bahamas with over fifty pieces of luggage on 17 August. They found themselves confronted with a formidable task. The normal trade of the islands was completely disrupted by the war; a mysterious disease had attacked the sponge fisheries; and hundreds of unemployed loitered in the streets and along the waterfront. The Duke rose to the challenge with commendable spirit. He persuaded an American firm to supervise the expansion of a fish packing plant; he obtained contracts for shipbuilding at Nassau; he established an Economic Investigation Committee; he immersed himself in welfare work for the natives, many of whom were found employment in the construction of a large air base. Despite the constant threat of German submarines and rumours of plots to take them hostage, he bought a cabin cruiser and, with the Duchess, visited nearly all the inhabited islands. The Duchess herself founded clinics for expectant mothers and young children, and organised a canteen where she put her talents as a cook to good use by preparing what she later estimated to be forty thousand plates of bacon and eggs in three years. Deservedly, both she and the Duke became extremely popular with the coloured population of the islands who knew that the Duke would have done much more for them had his suggestions for reforms, including the establishment of a minimum wage for workers, not met with such firm opposition from the die-hards in the Assembly. When the time came for him to leave the islands he had become, so one native West Indian admirer thought, one of the most respected Englishmen since Wilberforce.

13 The Duke of Windsor, in his role as Governor of
the Bahamas, visits Miami, Florida, in May 1941

1 / From Osborne to Flanders

'The risks will be accentuated by HRH's enthusiasm.'

'Now that you are leaving home, David, and going out into the world,' his father said to the thirteen-year-old Prince when taking him to the Royal Naval College at Osborne, 'always remember that I am your best friend.' In the months that followed the Prince might well have found difficulty in following this advice; for Osborne did not seem to him the kind of place to which one willingly despatched one's friends of any sort. His difficulties as a new boy, he later confessed, 'nearly overpowered' him. These difficulties would undoubtedly have been bad enough had he gone to a public school; but for a nervous, diffident, sensitive boy, who had not been away from home before and had had very little opportunity of mixing with children of his own age, Osborne held all the horrors of a 1907 public school with few of its advantages. There was no privacy: he was put into a dormitory with thirty other boys. There was no comfort: the meals were ill-cooked and inadequate. There was little friendship for him and much prejudiced distaste: he was called 'Sardine'. Apparently he was bullied by the bigger boys one of whom, for some infringement of the numerous perplexing rules that govern behaviour in such establishments, caught him by the collar and said, 'You are the Prince, are you? Well, learn to respect your seniors.' The reprimand was followed by a bottle of red ink being poured down his neck. On other occasions, he was held down over the window-sill while the sash was brought down on his neck to remind him of the block and the axe which had ended the life of at least one distant forebear. He settled down in the end, of course, in resignation if not in happiness; and the three months' cruise in the *Hindustan* in 1910 he found actually enjoyable. Nevertheless, he did not look back on his days as a naval cadet with any deep sense of pleasure. The Army was a different matter.

He trained with the Grenadier Guards at Wellington Barracks and Warley; and in October 1914, having been granted his commission, he went to ask the Secretary of State for War if he could go on active service. It would not matter if he were killed, he said; he had four brothers. No, Lord Kitchener agreed with characteristic bluntness, it would not much matter if he *were* killed, to be sure. But it would matter very much indeed if he were to be taken prisoner. So he could not go to France yet. Once a stabilized front had been established, the matter might be reconsidered.

Bitterly disappointed, the Prince went to see Sir Dighton Probyn, VC, who had served his grandfather for many years as Keeper of the Privy Purse, and tears came into his eyes as he asked the old general to intercede with Kitchener on his behalf. But Probyn could do nothing. The weeks passed; the Prince was kept waiting; he went to see Kitchener again; Kitchener repeated his refusal. Then at last, after the front had been stabilized by the first battle of Ypres, he was given a staff appointment and allowed to sail.

14 Queen Victoria at Osborne in 1900 with four great-grandchildren, Mary, Edward (centre), Henry, Duke of Gloucester, and George (on cushion)

15 In February 1896 Edward's brother, who became George VI, was born; they were photographed with their mother in 1898

16 Sailor suits were the fashion; Edward was photographed in one when his father was captain of H.M.S. Crescent

17 (Below) George V, with fashionable cigarette, holds the hand of Henry. Edward is in the middle, Mary and George on his right (1902)

Those who were to be responsible for him did not relish the thought of his arrival. They feared, with due cause, that he would be more of a liability than a help to them, that it would be difficult to keep him out of danger. 'The risks', one officer complained to the King's Private Secretary, 'will be accentuated by HRH's enthusiasm.' The King himself thought it as well to assure Lord Cavan, commander of the Guards Division, that neither he nor Brigadier Gathorne-Hardy would 'be held responsible for his personal safety'. 'Of course risks there must be,' the King's Secretary conceded. 'We can only hope and pray that all will be well and His Majesty feels that this change will be good for the Prince and also that his occasional presence forward will be appreciated by the men.'

Risks there certainly were. In September 1915 Lord Cavan gave the King a report of a tour of inspection he had made with the Prince along the front at Vermelles. When they returned to their cars, which had been left behind the trenches under cover, they found that they had been torn apart by shrapnel. The Prince's driver, who had been in his service since his Oxford days, was dead.

On several occasions the Prince went up to the front without authority. On one of these Sir Charles Munro, the First Army Corps Commander, felt obliged to follow him. He found the Prince and beckoned to him. The Prince 'somewhat reluctantly came to the side of the car', mumbling under his breath. 'I heard what you said, Prince,' said Sir Charles, ' "Here is that damned old General after me again!" Jump into the car, or you will spoil my appetite for breakfast.'

Another general, Sir Frederick Maude, found him equally tiresome. 'Thank Heavens he's going,' Maude said when the Prince was transferred to another command. 'This job will turn my hair grey. . . . He insists on tramping in the front lines.'

The Prince was transferred several times and gave the same sort of trouble wherever he went, though the men in the lines which he visited were always pleased to see him. 'He had a roving commission of which he took full advantage,' recalls Rupert Grayson, then a young officer in the Irish Guards. 'He moved among the troops from one end of our lines to the other. He was a familiar and much-loved figure.' After various staff appointments in France, he went to Egypt where he demonstrated his impatience with the lack of activity there, and his boredom with a report that he had been asked to prepare on the Suez Canal, by driving a golf ball from the top of one of the pyramids. And from Egypt he went to the Italian front where he and King Victor Emmanuel II 'were all the time warning each other not to take risks', so a British liaison officer reported. 'The King was afraid of the Prince's daily habit of going too near to the Austrian lines. When the Prince went back to Italy in 1918 to stay with the King, he broke away from all warnings and control and flew over the Austrian trenches. . . . The King was perturbed and almost angry at the bravado of his guest.'

*18 By 1905 there were six children for this photograph
taken at Abergeldie Castle, Aberdeenshire. The
princeling was John*

19 'Self and Bertie' at Sandringham, 1905. Together
   Edward and George helped to build a new reservoir

20 *Edward captioned this picture in his album: 'Bertie and I on the beach at Osborne Bay', 1906*   21 *Edward aloft in the bos'n's chair in a yacht off Cowes, 1906*

22 *In July 1906 Edward went on a choir treat from the Royal Naval College, Osborne, to Alum Bay, Isle of Wight*

23 *By 1908 Edward had been two years at the Royal Naval College, and he was in this uniform the only time he met Uncle Nicky, Czar Nicholas of Russia, who visited Cowes in August 1908. Edward VII is seated centre, between the Czar and the Czarina. Edward is on the left of the group*

24 *(Left) Three sailor kings together, 1908: Edward VII is seated between George V and Edward VIII*

25 *Driving to Craithie from Balmoral with bearded French master, M. Hua: 1909*

26 *Edward with Monsieur Hua and George*

27 *Queen Mary with her naval cadet sons at Barton Manor, Osborne, 1909*

28 *'Grandpapa' shortly before his death in 1910*

29 *The new King, George V, Edward, George (in sailor*
    suits), the Kaiser, the Duke of Connaught, the King
    of Spain, and the King of Bulgaria, walk through
    Windsor in the funeral procession of Edward VII,
    1910

Edward, right, and his brothers watch the proclamation of their father as King at St James's Palace, 1910

(Below left) The coronation portrait of Edward's parents

32 *(Below right) Conscious of new responsibilities Edward salutes the crowds in London as he leaves in an open landau with his mother, Queen Mary, 1911*

33 *With Princess Mary, Queen Mary, and John, Edward
visits the Crystal Palace in 1911*

34 *(Right) In 1911 Edward became Prince of Wales.
King George V takes Edward's hand to present him to
the Welsh nation*

35 Edward, now Prince of Wales, was still a midshipman on H.M.S. Hindustan in 1911

37 (Below) Golf was to become his passion: Edward with George and their tutor, H. P. Hansell, at Newquay

36 Edward met W. G. Grace in 1911 but, despite a long talk with him, never took to cricket

*38 Three tutors oversee the education of the Royal
     children, 1911*

39 *A self-conscious cigarette: 'Now that I was eighteen,' Edward later wrote, 'my father allowed me to smoke'*

41 *(Right) Edward captioned this 'Self with 1st stag'*

40 *In 1912 Edward was photographed with his first pipe whilst wading with his brothers in Loch Muick near Balmoral*

42 *Sightseeing in France, 1912*

44 *Walking with his tutor, H. P. Hansell, in Paris*

43 *Although Edward travelled as the Earl of Chester to relieve the French Government of protocol difficulties, formalities still existed. Here he is met at Calais station by the British consul, Mr Paignton*

45 *At the Oval, Kennington, with his tutor and his brother George*

46

46 Edward in Germany, with his uncle Prince Henry of Prussia. In 1913 he visited the Kaiser's younger brother at his home near Kiel

48 'Mary at her window': by 1913 Edward was a keen photographer

47 Following the 1913 University boat race from the Judges' launch

49 Another photograph of his sister: 'I took this picture at Buckingham Palace,' Edward wrote

50 1913: as a member of the Oxford University O.T.C.,
Edward marches back from a field day, with his rifle
slung over his shoulder

51 *March 1914: Edward winter-sporting at Voksenkollen in Norway*   52 *At the O.T.C. Camp at Farnborough, the same year*

Self.

Self.

53 *On manoeuvres as a corporal at Hartford Bridge Flats, in Hampshire, 1914*

54 *Resting in the Camp*

55 *It was Lord Kitchener (foreground) who initially blocked Edward's entry to the Army when war broke out, claiming that it was not the death of the Prince that mattered but his capture which would be embarrassing*

56 *But once the front line had settled down, Edward was allowed to join up*

*57 Edward with Major Thompson, watching the
departure from Calais of S.S. Invicta with George V
on board, 15. August 1916*

*58 Edward with his parents, Sir Douglas Haig (behind)
and M. Poincaré, at Abbeville, 1917*

*59 Armistice Day, 1918: Edward, then a major, with
Haig at the Allied Advanced General H.Q. at Iwuy
in France*

*60 On the Italian Front in 1918 with Lord Cavan,
    awaiting the arrival of the Allied commanders*

2/Around the World

'This smiling, appealing youthful man.'

In the course of his varied service in the First World War, the Prince had come into contact with men from all over the Empire, the Dominions and the United States. He had bathed in the Suez Canal with soldiers from Australia and New Zealand; he had been attached to the Australian Corps Headquarters at Ham and to the New Zealand Division Headquarters at Leverkusen: he had spent some time at the United States Army Headquarters at Coblenz and with General Pershing's staff at Chaumont; and he had been piloted over the Rhine by General 'Billy' Mitchell, the American Air Force commander; at the time of the Armistice he was with the Canadian Corps. He had found most of the officers and men he had met highly agreeable, and had been heartened by their assurances of a warm welcome whenever he visited their homelands.

He was not disappointed. He sailed the Atlantic in HMS *Renown* in August 1919, soon after his twenty-fifth birthday. He was in excellent spirits throughout the voyage. 'Every day HRH inspected some part of the ship, and we had some of the officers to lunch or dinner,' one of his companions recorded; 'very enjoyable, informal meals they were, too, without any special ceremony. . . . HRH kept up the old naval custom of proposing the health of "sweethearts and wives". . . . . The Prince and his staff dined in the wardroom, and we had a semi-organised "rag" afterwards – quite the leading spirit being HRH who finished the evening about 12.30 a.m. looking very hot and dishevelled, rather dirty about the shirt-sleeves and with something round his neck that might once have been a collar.'

Although his welcome in Canada was certainly warm, his tour of the country was exhausting. He travelled over ten thousand miles, made over a hundred speeches, shook hands with so many mayors and other dignitaries that by the time he left Toronto his right hand was so sore he could not bear to have it touched any more, and his left hand, too, was strained. Nevertheless, having agreed to buy a ranch at Calgary, and having delighted Canadians by riding a bucking bronco at a rodeo, he wanted to go on to the United States before returning home.

His reception in New York was tumultuous; confetti and ticker tape and bits of telephone directories poured down upon his car from the windows of New York; and the people cheered him in the streets as though he were a returning hero. He looked a little bewildered, and astonishingly young for twenty-five. It was noticed how nervously he fingered his tie and smoothed his fair hair; but wherever he went most Americans were as evidently delighted with him as he seemed to be with them. The British government was also delighted; and plans were made to send him away on another tour of goodwill soon after his return to England.

61 Edward on the cowcatcher of the train in which he
crossed Canada, 1919

So, by way of Barbados, Honolulu and Fiji, he sailed for New Zealand and Australia. Although he had been in tears on the day of his departure, here too he enjoyed a personal triumph. Conscientiously he shook hands, smiled, waved, raised his grey felt hat, made polite speeches, asked questions; and the people were charmed by him. He still picked at his tie and fidgeted and smoked cigarettes incessantly. Yet, though he was remarkably immature for his years, he was undoubtedly an attractive young man, interested and concerned; and there was about him a certain magnetism which had much to do with his being Prince of Wales but owed something, too, to the power of his own personality. 'Before the Prince landed the popular idea of princes was of something haughty and remote,' according to the *Sydney Sun*, 'but this smiling, appealing youthful man smiled away the differences which Australians believed lay between' royalty and the common people. Other newspapers reported how his train had been derailed on its way to Perth; his carriage had overturned, and his staff had crawled out of the windows shocked and scratched. For some time the Prince did not appear. When at length he did so, he explained that he had had to gather up his papers. He thanked the anxious and apologetic Australian officials for providing him with an interesting experience not listed on the official programme, and later apologised to the guests in Perth who were waiting for him to join a lunch party without giving them any reason for his being late. By the end of the tour he was utterly exhausted; and his cousin, Lord Louis Mountbatten, who had accompanied him, well knew what a strain it had been for him and that 'under that delightful smile which charmed people everywhere . . . he was a lonely and sad person, always liable to deep depressions.' For days on end he had been unable to bring himself to face anyone other than Lord Louis or even to finish his meals.

Returning to England by way of the West Indies, the Prince was told he must set sail again almost immediately, this time for India. He dreaded the thought of going away so soon, of leaving Mrs Dudley Ward, abandoning all the pleasures of England and submitting himself yet again to the exacting duties of an ambassador. His father, however, was insistent. 'I don't care whether the PM wants you to go or not. *I* wish you to go, and you are going.'

The Prince managed to postpone the date of his departure for a few months. But in October 1921 he sailed from England once more. In India he travelled over forty thousand miles, from Bombay to Baroda, north to Udaipur, from there to Bikaner, across the Ganges to Lucknow and Benares, on to Patna, Calcutta, Mandalay and Rangoon, from Madras to Mysore, Gwalior and Delhi, from Lahore and Jammu over the plains of Afghanistan, back to Rawalpindi and Karachi. And from Karachi he sailed down to Ceylon and then to Malaya.

It was not only a difficult and tiring journey, it was also frequently a disconcerting and alarming one. For Gandhi had called for a boycott of the tour and had greeted the Prince's arrival in Bombay by supervising a public burning of foreign clothes, by urging the people to remain indoors, close their shops and to display placards condemning the royal visit. In many places Gandhi's pleas were highly effective. In Bombay his placards were displayed in their thousands 'in every nook and corner of the city' and hundreds of white Gandhi caps were to be seen in every street. At Agra 'No welcome to the Prince' was scrawled across the shutters of the closed shops. At Calcutta, where thousands of people stayed indoors and the jeers almost drowned the cheering, the Prince's reception was described by Lord Rawlinson as a 'fiasco'. In Madras the decorations were torn down, windows were smashed, pictures of the Prince were stamped underfoot, a cinema was set on fire. There would have been similar demonstrations elsewhere had not many of Gandhi's supporters been arrested as they were at Benares.

Yet even in those places where opposition to the royal visit was most vehement, the Prince succeeded in winning people over by what the British Resident at Baroda called his 'unfailing charm and sincerity of manner'. The Prince's reception at Baroda, despite the 'large number of Gandhi caps', was 'considered exceptionally enthusiastic by people of long Baroda experience', the Resident reported to the Political Secretary. 'Politically both in respect of State and general situation, visit has been triumphal success, of which his Royal Highness's personality has been outstanding feature and main cause.' After the Prince's visit to Delhi, Lord Rawlinson recorded in his journal, 'The Prince's visit has gone off splendidly which is tremendous relief. He has worked very hard. His winning smile and extraordinarily attractive manner won the hearts of all. He had another great success with a speech in Hindustani, which he learned by heart, to the 11th and 16th Rajputs. The men were delighted and cheered him to the echo.'

62 *In the post-war world there were fears that the links with the Empire were loosening, and Edward was sent on the first of his great overseas tours. He became his country's Ambassador Extraordinary. On the Nipigon in Canada, 1919*

64 *Cowboy country: at the Bar U Ranch, Canada*

65 *(Right) 'Chief Morning Star'*

63 *Flowers for the Prince in Courtney, Canada*

66 (Left) A famous and engaging photograph of Edward in the U.S.A., 1919

67 Sorting out calves for branding at the Bar U Ranch

68 Enormous crowds gathered wherever Edward went in Canada: Brantford railway station, 1919

69 (Overleaf) Back at the Ranch

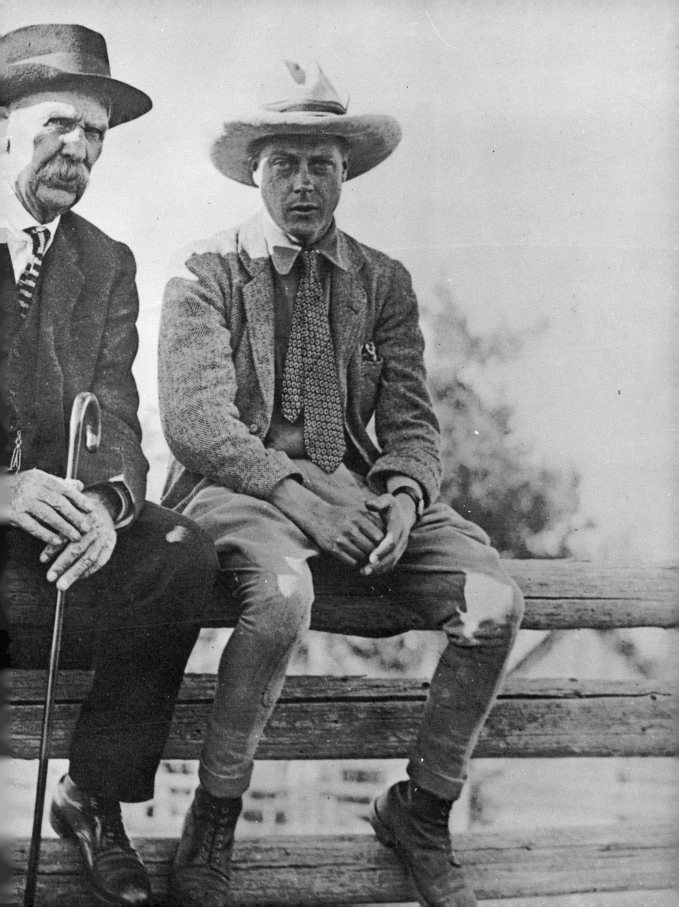

70 *By the time Edward entered the U.S.A. in November 1919, his right hand was so crushed that he was unable to use it, and he shook hands with his left instead. Annapolis, 1919*

71 *A visit to the Cymner coalmine in Wales, also in 1919*

72 *(Right) A visit to Lloyd's with his brother in the same year*

73 *(Overleaf) Taking the salute of Australian troops on Anzac Day, 1919*

74 In March 1920 Edward set off again to see more of the Empire. Seeing him off are (left to right) Henry, George, and Lord Louis Mountbatten

75 Chatting with a West Indian sergeant

76 Inspecting a band of the Barbados Volunteers

77 *Submitting to the barber on the way to Australasia*

78 *(Below) Inspecting the guard of the Fijian Constabulary at Suva*

79 *Presenting the King's Police Medal for heroism to a Fijian policeman*

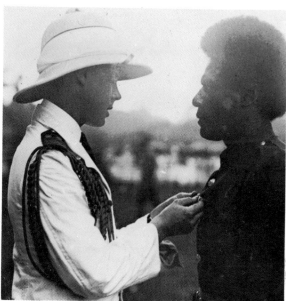

*82 In Bendigo, Victoria, Edward went down a goldmine
with the Australian Prime Minister, W. H. Hughes*

83 *Trying his hand at wood-chopping at the Pemberton State Saw Mills, 1920*

84 *Reviewing the Boy Scouts in Sydney*

85 *Laying the foundation stone of the new federal capital, Canberra, in 1920*

86 *Another meeting with the Australian Prime Minister*

*87 In September the tour ended. A group of Sydney
ladies visit the* Renown *to say farewell*

88 *Edward wins his first race under National Hunt rules, 1921 – and is the occasion for a rare display of jollity on the part of Queen Mary*

89 *Kicking off the Tottenham Hotspur and Fulham match, 1921*

90 *The ceremony of the unveiling of the Cenotaph*

91 *Talking to Australian cricket captain, Warwick Armstrong, at Bristol in 1921*

On tour again, this time in the Far East: in Nepal,
Edward (extreme right) took part in a formal tiger
shoot, 1922

93 *'Tell Daddy we are all happy under British rule.'*
Aden, November, 1921

95 *In the uniform of 35th and 26th Jacobs Horses, of*
which Edward was Colonel-in-Chief, India, 1922

94 *(Below) A wheelbarrow race in Malta, 1921: Lord*
Mountbatten at the helm

96 *Edward walking with Her Majesty, the Begum of Bhopal*

97 *Duck netting at the Hamam Palace in Tokyo, 1922: preliminary practice with a tennis ball*

98 *Hong Kong, 1922: a little help from the Chinese*

99 *A buckled rickshaw wheel – the result of over-energetic exertions by Edward during a climb to Lake Chuzeriji. Admiral Halsey is the passenger*

100 *Before leaving Japan, Edward, with his staff, was photographed in Japanese costume, 1922*

101 *(Below) The homecoming: posing with Edward are (left to right) Queen Mary, Henry, George, George V, Lord Lascelles and Mary*

102 *Edward, Mary and George at the wedding of their cousin Lord Mountbatten to Lady Edwina Ashley*

103 *Edward had gained world-wide popularity with his Far East tour which was reflected in a new-found confidence at home. Edward attends a Boy Scout rally at Alexandria Palace, 1922*

104 *Polo-playing at Hurlingham, 1923*

105 *When riding with his father in Windsor Great Park, no risks were taken*

106 *The fellowship of hunting*

107 *(Left) Edward receives a wetting at the water jump during the Arborfield Cross point-to-point, 1924*

108 *At the first fence his horse, Little Favourite, fell (see page 20). Edward was concussed and had to be carried off the field. His father forbade him to steeplechase again*

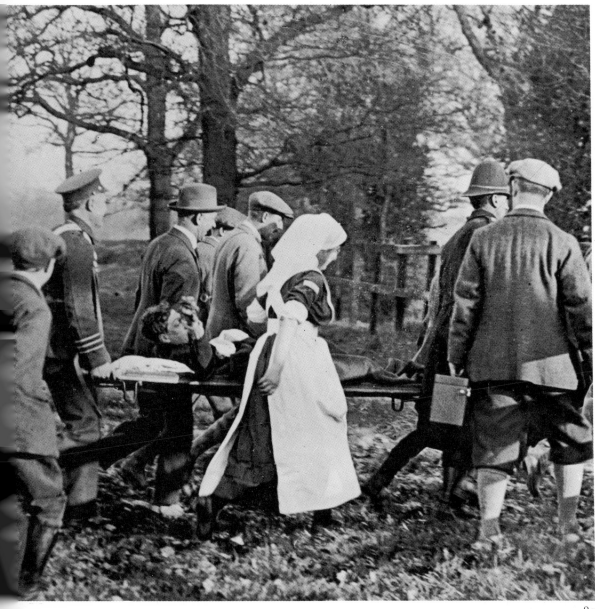

109 *In July 1924 no one was more qualified than*
   Edward to visit the British Empire Exhibition at
   Wembley

110 *In August Edward went to the U.S.A. for a second*
   visit. In November he and his father met the
   players of the Chicago team in a baseball match at
   Stamford Bridge

3 / Africa and America

'The air rang with cheers.'

It was not only the Prince's charm, his evident anxiety to please, his unaffected nature and easy informality which had been admired by the Indians, but also his bravery. As his by no means fulsome biographer, Hector Bolitho, has said, his courage was 'tremendous'. 'Most of the time he was travelling in danger and the guards which surrounded him were necessary. In the columns of the Indian newspapers one does not find stories of an anxious traveller, looking this way and that as he wrestled with the hartals [non-violent protests] which Gandhi had prepared for him.' After the demonstrations against him at Madras he walked down from the stand on the race-course and strolled into the public enclosure. 'This was a daring thing to do and the mass of people were amazed. They parted to make way for him. For a moment they could not believe that he was among them; then the air rang with cheers.'

No one was in the least surprised when the Prince admitted at Delhi that every single night when he went to bed he was 'dog tired'. But it was not until he had made a tour of Japan that he sailed home again.

Even then he did not remain in England for long. In 1925 he was required to sail away once more, this time to South Africa by way of the Gold Coast and Nigeria where he reviewed twenty thousand horsemen in a great durbar on the Kano Plain. In South Africa he made more speeches, waved to more people gathered beside the railway tracks, shook thousands more hands, travelled thousands more miles, inspected more farms and factories, reviewed more regiments, danced and dined, looked pensive and sad – and smiled. There were occasional lapses, flashes of impatience and irritability. There had been a story that in Canada, when a mayor began an only too familiar speech with the words, 'Not only do we welcome your Royal Highness as the representative of his Majesty the King, but we . . .', then came to a halt as he lost his place in his muddled notes, the Prince continued for him by wearily whispering, 'We welcome you for *yourself.*' In South Africa, the Prince went further than this. At the end of an excessively long speech by the mayor of a small town, he rolled up the paper on which his own speech had been written, handed it to the mayor and told him that he could read it afterwards to himself. These lapses were rare, however. Most of the time in South Africa, and during a subsequent tour of South America, the Prince behaved tactfully and with circumspection. There were well-founded rumours that he was sometimes distressingly ill-mannered at the evening entertainments provided for him, dancing all night with the prettiest girls in the room, while ignoring his hostesses. There were also stories of his having snubbed people for being too familiar with him, though it was he himself who had encouraged them to be so. But when on duty in the day time he

112 Edward in the Chicago stockyards with Louis J. Swift, 1924

was usually polite and sympathetic, and as conscientious as ever, still deserving the title which Lloyd George bestowed on him as 'our greatest ambassador'.

He was, nevertheless, finding the burden of such a responsibility increasingly tiring and irksome. He once wrote in his diary, 'What rot and a waste of time, money, and energy all these state visits are!! This is my only remark on all this unreal show and ceremony.' By the time of his second visit to the United States, which had taken place in 1924, he had grown thoroughly impatient with convention and protocol, and considered with due cause that he had by now earned the right to enjoy himself with more abandon.

In America he certainly did enjoy himself; and the American press reported his activities in much detail and with some asperity. 'He managed, by his choice of friends and diversions,' one New York paper wrote, 'to provoke an exhibition of social climbing on the part of a few Americans which has added nothing to his prestige nor to the prestige of royalty in general. A good deal of hot fuel is added to the fires of the old-fashioned Republican conviction that civilisation would survive if the King business were wound up.'

At home his father was aghast at the reports about him; and when the Prince returned, he found the King's desk littered with newspaper clippings: 'Did you see this when you were in New York?' the King asked him, holding up one headline: '*Prince gets in with milkman.*' Other clippings were produced from the file, '*Here he is girls – the most eligible bachelor yet uncaught.*' '*Oh! Who'll ask HRH what he wears asleep?*' '*Prince of Wales has 'em guessing in the wee hours.*'

But if the Prince were, indeed, the 'most eligible bachelor yet uncaught', he had as yet, so far as his father knew, entertained no thoughts of marriage. When he did do so he could not bring himself to break the news to him. He thought of doing so at Sandringham during the Christmas holiday of 1935; but the King looked so old and ill and bent, that the Prince could not bear to raise a matter which would certainly distress him beyond measure. Before another opportunity presented itself King George V was dead.

113 *With the President of Argentina at a ball on board H.M.S.* Eagle *at Buenos Aires, 1931, during Edward's second visit to South America*

114 *In March 1925 Edward set off in the H.M.S.*
Repulse to visit Africa and South America. In
June the Mayor of Johannesburg welcomed him to
the golden city

115 *Inspecting prize cattle at the Royal Agricultural*
Show, Pietermaritzburg

*116 Receiving homage in Accra from chiefs of the Central
and Eastern provinces of the Gold Coast (now
Ghana)*

117 *(Left) Edward lays the foundation stone of the George Canning monument in Santiago*

118 *Inaugurating a hydro-electric power scheme at Broken Hill in Northern Rhodesia*

119 *En route for Government House with the President of Argentina*

120 *A visit to Napoleon's Tomb, August 1925*

121 *Edward and staff photographed with the ship's company of H.M.S. Repulse on the voyage home from South America. October 1925*

122 Most of Edward's travels were by sea or rail, but the coming of the aeroplane was to make things quicker. In 1927 he had a close look at one on his visit to Spain. Like riding, air travel was something his father disapproved of

123 (Below) In 1928 there was need for additional care. George V was seriously ill. On his partial recovery he drove to Bognor to recuperate. The whole of the back of the ambulance was of glass, so that George V could be seen by his subjects

124 Edward opens the Newcastle Exhibition, 1929

125 (Right) Queen Mary at her husband's side during his convalescence at Bognor Regis

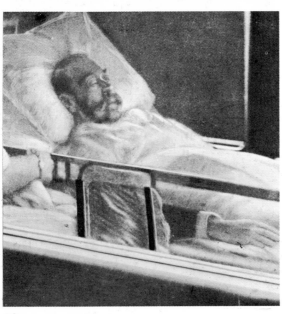

126 *(Left) In 1930 Edward fell for Fort Belvedere near Sunningdale and used it as a haven from official duties*

127 *There were, it might appear, enough guns to defy the world*

128 *The swimming pool and the cairn terriers gavè particular delight*

*130 At Llanelli Edward shakes hands with a V.C.
holder at the Royal Welsh Agricultural Show*

131 *In 1932 Edward was in the Mediterranean, August found him on the Venice Lido with Captain Alistair Mackintosh*

132 *In September Edward was in Hamburg*

133 *(Right) In June 1933 Edward was at Ascot*

134 *Edward tags along behind Queen Mary at a garden
party at Buckingham Palace*

135 *Distributing leeks to the officers and men of the Welsh Guards at Chelsea Barracks, St David's Day 1935*

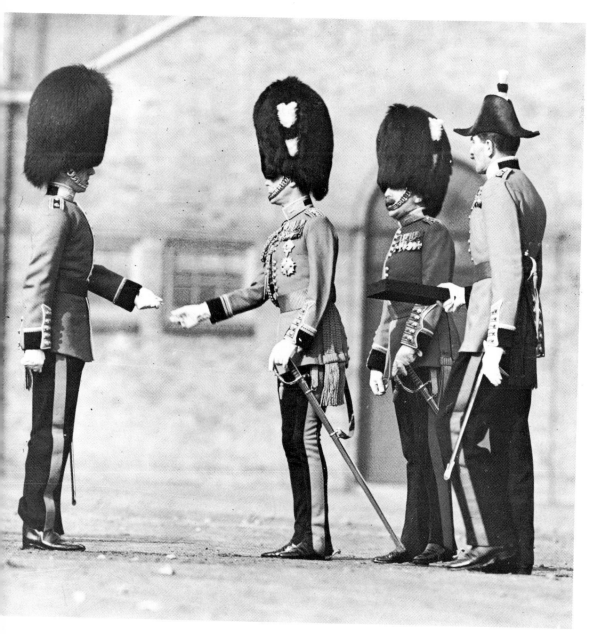

136 *Riding with the King and George at the Trooping of the Colour, June 1934*

137 *(Below) At Balmoral with his nieces, Margaret and Elizabeth*

138 *Edward and George at Portsmouth to greet their brother Henry on his return to England aboard H.M.S.* Australia, *March 1935*

*139 1935 was Silver Jubilee year: the King and Queen
photographed at prayer in St Paul's on 6 May*

140 *The Jubilee review of the Fleet at Spithead in July:*
Edward and his father together with George and the
Duke of Kent

141 *Edward kisses Queen Mary's hand as she arrives at*
Eton during the Jubilee drive to Windsor

142 *(Right) The Jubilee party on the balcony of*
Buckingham Palace in May

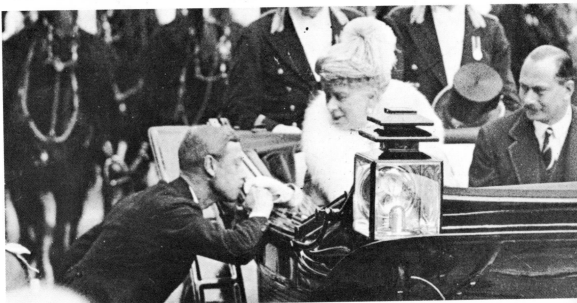

143 *(Left) Queen Mary's official Jubilee portrait, 1935*

144 *King George V died on 20 January 1936. On 23 January the four royal brothers followed their father's coffin from the church at Sandringham*

145 In the funeral procession, on 29 January 1936, Edward, the new king, walked ahead of his three brothers

146 (Right) The late King's lying-in-state in Westminster Hall

4/Abdication Overture

'The most serious crisis of my life.'

At Fort Belvedere, on the evening of 13 November 1936, King Edward VIII was confronted by what he described as 'the most serious crisis' of his life. It was a letter from his Private Secretary marked 'urgent and confidential'. Its contents left him 'shocked and angry' For Major Alexander Hardinge had felt it his duty to bring to his Majesty the following facts which he *knew* to be accurate:

1. The silence of the British press on the subject of your Majesty's friendship with Mrs Simpson is *not* going to be maintained. It is probably only a matter of days before the outburst begins. Judging by the letters from British subjects living in foreign countries where the press has been outspoken, the effect will be calamitous.

2. The Prime Minister and senior members of the Government are meeting today to discuss what actions should be taken to deal with the serious situation which is developing. As Your Majesty no doubt knows the resignation of the Government – an eventuality which can by no means be excluded – would result in Your Majesty having to find someone else capable of forming a Government which would receive the support of the present House of Commons. I have reason to know that, in view of the feeling prevalent among members of the House of Commons of all parties, this is hardly within the bounds of possibility. . . .

If your Majesty will permit me to say so, there is only one step which holds out any prospect of avoiding this dangerous situation, and that is for Mrs Simpson to go abroad *without further delay.*

As the King suspected, Hardinge had written this letter after consultations with the Prime Minister who, by now, had had the opportunity of estimating the nature and strength of opinion both within Parliament and in the country at large. Baldwin was satisfied that there could be no question of Mrs Simpson becoming Queen. This, of course, was the opinion of the Establishment. Mrs Simpson, it was generally admitted, was charming and intelligent. It was also generally admitted, though without so much conviction, that being an American woman of no distinguished lineage did not necessarily render her unsuitable for the position to which the King wanted to raise her. But what could not be denied was that her having two former husbands living would have to be regarded as an insuperable obstacle to the King's hopes. It was not only the Court and Cabinet, the Queen Mother, the Church and Geoffrey Dawson who held this view. So did Mackenzie King, speaking on behalf of Canadian public opinion; so did Stanley Bruce, representing Australia; so did Sir Walter Citrine, general secretary of the Trades Union Congress; so did Clement Attlee, leader of the Labour Party.

The King, however, had good grounds for believing that in a clash with the Government the British people would for the most part be on his side. They had recently heard on the

147 The new King at the Trooping of the Colour, June 1936

wireless the enthusiastic cheers with which he had so warmly been greeted at the Albert Hall on Armistice night; and they had read in the papers how at dawn the next morning he had embarked on a highly successful inspection of the Fleet. He had returned to Fort Belvedere, exhilarated by his experiences, to be confronted and angered by Hardinge's letter. He took it, as he later confessed, as a 'challenge'.

He sent for his old friend Walter Monckton who agreed to act as a go-between in the negotiations which could now no longer be delayed. He also sent for the two members of the Government whom he felt would have most sympathy for his position, Samuel Hoare and Duff Cooper. Both, indeed, were sympathetic; but neither was encouraging. Hoare, 'acutely conscious of the political realities', warned the King that Baldwin had the wholehearted backing of the Cabinet. Duff Cooper could merely advocate delay. 'I thought that if they would agree not to meet for a year, during which he would be crowned,' Duff Cooper wrote in his memoirs, 'he would at the end of that period have grown more accustomed to his position and more loath to leave it. I also secretly thought that he might in the interval meet somebody whom he would love more. He never has. He refused to consider the suggestion for a reason which did him credit. He felt it would be wrong to go through so solemn a religious ceremony as the coronation without letting his subjects know what it was his intention to do.'

'Whatever the cost to me personally,' the King commented, 'I was determined, before I would think of being crowned, to settle once and for all the question of my right to marry.'

It was a decision that was to cost him the throne.

148 On board the yacht 'Nahlin' in the summer of 1936: during this cruise Edward decided to turn the Establishment upside down

149 'Though as I now speak as King, I am still that same man better known to most of my listeners as Prince of Wales,' Edward pronounced. The routine of royalty remained much the same. Here the King drives in state to Buckingham Palace

150 (Below) Edward had been proclaimed king on 22 January. Clarenceux King of Arms read the Royal Proclamation on the steps of the Royal Exchange. Mr and Mrs Simpson were with Edward at St James's Palace to watch the ceremony of proclamation

151 Edward, touring the Duchy of Cornwall, arrives at Princetown on 3 June, 1936

152 (Right) A visit to the Queen Mary at Clydebank

153 On 16 July Edward presented new colours in Hyde Park to six battalions of the Foot Guards. On his way back to Buckingham Palace a loaded revolver fell at his feet. A mounted policeman picked it up (bottom right), and the assailant, George Andrew MacMahon, was hustled past the St John Ambulance (left centre). MacMahon claimed to be suffering from an injustice and wished only to call attention to it. Later, on trial at the Central Criminal Court, he claimed to be an assassin hired by a foreign power. Whatever the truth, Edward was unlikely to forget that the incident happened at almost the same spot on Constitution Hill where Queen Victoria had been shot at

154 *'This picture of me as King was thought by some to be too informal,' said Edward, who recalled an M.P. saying, 'We can't have the King doing this kind of thing. He has the Daimler'*

155 *For those in the know, the burning question concerned Mrs Simpson. How would his new status affect their relationship? In the summer of 1934 there had been sensational American newspaper reports of a yachting cruise which Edward was making in the Mediterranean with an American divorcee guest. Here they pose on a rock in a lonely part of Corsica*

156 *(Below) In February 1935 they were photographed together ski-ing at Kitzbühl*

*157 and 158 The summer of 1934: Edward's own
   photographs of Wallis Simpson and Pookie*

159 *The summer of 1935: another cruise in the Mediterranean. Mrs Simpson was again one of the guests on the Duke of Westminster's yacht. Edward's shadow falls across the picture of Wallis on the island of Porquerelles off the South Coast of France*

160 *Edward in turn is photographed*

161 *Another snapshot of Wallis on Porquerelles*

162 *The summer of 1936: on board Lady Yule's yacht 'Nahlin', which Edward hired for an Adriatic cruise*

163–167 *The first British press photographs of Edward and Mrs Simpson together were taken by Jarche, the famous photographer of* Illustrated *magazine. 'I used a miniature camera,' Jarche recalled. The scene is Cochrane's cabaret in the Grosvenor House Hotel, three months before the abdication*

168 *The King photographed in the company of Mrs Simpson and Lord Mountbatten*

169 *A place in the sun: near Cannes, 1936*

170 and 171 (right) The cruise of the 'Nahlin' continues. Although the British press maintained silence and Jarche's pictures were not published, the summer of '36 was perhaps decisive in Edward's relationship with Mrs Simpson

172 (Below left) Sightseeing at Tregir, near Split, on the Dalmatian coast, 1936

*74 **This triumphal photograph by Edward symbolises
the happy and relaxed quality of their relationship,
but they were soon to return to mounting tension and
challenge at home***

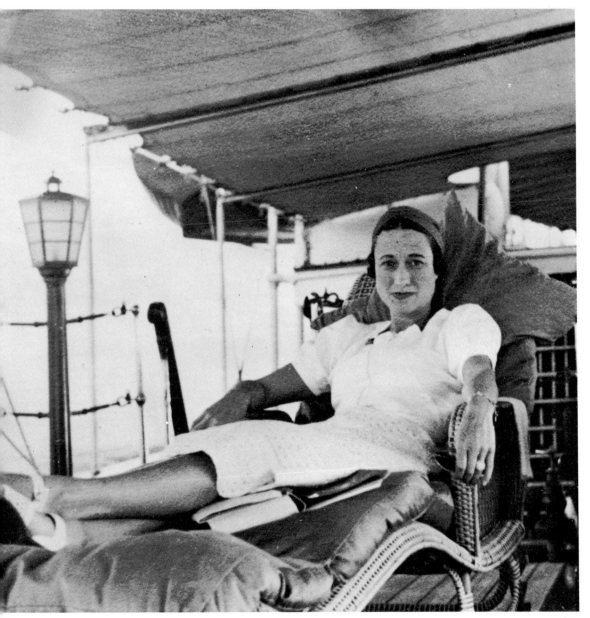

175 *On 7 September Edward rode with Kemal Ataturk*
     through the streets of Istanbul

*176 In Austria Edward got his eye in, shooting
partridges on the estate of Sir Walford Selby, the
British Ambassador to Austria*

177 *Towards the end of September Edward and guests*
made the customary pilgrimage to Balmoral. But the
guests were not all from the customary establishment;
they included Mrs Simpson

178 Together the King and Mrs Simpson pose by a
waterfall at Balmoral

178 Together the King and Mrs Simpson pose by a
waterfall at Balmoral

5 / Finale

'The country as a whole was getting progressively more shocked.'

Soon after his inconclusive discussions with Duff Cooper, the King went away on his celebrated visit to South Wales, a visit which had been planned many weeks before. As on previous visits to distressed industrial areas he was clearly moved by the poverty he witnessed, and frustrated by the limitations imposed on his ability to do anything about it. His assurance to an unemployed miner, 'Something must be done . . . and I will do all I can to assist you,' was repeated all over the country and was widely taken to be a condemnation of the government's inadequacy. It was hailed as representing the feelings of a man who was to be praised at the time of his death by one of his family's most outspoken critics, William Hamilton, the Labour Member for West Fife, as 'the most radical sovereign in centuries', a king who would be remembered 'by many not usually sympathetic to the monarchy as a man more sensitive to the needs and thoughts of ordinary folk than any other monarch they have known or read about'.

In fact, though undeniably compassionate and impatient of convention, the King was far from being a radical. In many respects he was as patrician in his outlook as his father; and at the time of the General Strike of 1926 had shown himself to be a good deal less forbearing in his attitude towards what he then evidently took to be the unreasonable aspirations of the poor. Nor were his remarks in South Wales in November 1936 entirely welcomed by the Labour Party. Herbert Morrison did not think well of them, since they were 'a case of a sovereign expressing views on matters which were the subject of political controversy'; while Aneurin Bevan refused to be associated with a visit which 'would appear to support the notion that private charity has made, or can ever make, a contribution of any value to the solution of the problems of South Wales.' Ernest Bevin was 'sorry that the King [had] been brought into this business'.

In the popular press, on the other hand, the King's stock rose to new heights. The *Daily Mirror*, for instance, contrasted the reaction of 'our beloved King', 'a wisely unconventional monarch', to the problems of South Wales with the indolence of Baldwin. Beaverbrook urged the King to take advantage of this upsurge of support by allowing newspapers to attack the government, to 'strike back vigorously' at Baldwin and his supporters who were endeavouring to deprive him of his throne. But the King was reluctant to do so. He wanted to 'dampen the uproar', as he put it; 'to avoid the responsibility of splitting the nation and jeopardizing the monarchy on the issue of [his] personal happiness; and to protect [Mrs Simpson] from the full blast of sensationalism.'

Already the celebrated speech of the Bishop of Bradford criticizing the King's behaviour had ended the press's uneasy silence about Mrs Simpson. Initial comments had been very

181 George, Duke of York – shortly to be George VI – arriving at his home, 145 Piccadilly, at the height of the abdication crisis

137

guarded; but the King dreaded the appearance of harmful and scandalous disclosures. He felt much more inclined to favour the idea, which Mrs Simpson herself suggested, that he should put his own point of view forward in a frank broadcast talk to the nation. There was 'no want of evidence', as he said, that 'a multitude of the plain people stood waiting to be rallied' to his side.

The Cabinet, however, did not feel able to agree to this suggestion. Nor did they feel able to agree to another proposal which had been made to them, a proposal originally made to Mrs Simpson by Esmond Harmsworth while the King was in Wales. This was that they might consider a morganatic marriage (in which the wife retains her lower rank and any offspring are debarred from the succession).

Mrs Simpson was not very taken with the idea which she thought might lead the King into a trap; but the King, believing it might be the only possible solution, asked Baldwin what he thought of it. Baldwin replied that he considered it unlikely that Parliament would pass the necessary Bill, but that if the King wanted him to do so, he would put the proposal before the Cabinet and the Prime Ministers of the Dominions. The King instructed him to go ahead; and from that moment the problem was resolved.

The Cabinet unanimously declined to agree to a morganatic marriage; the Prime Ministers of the Dominions were also universal in their condemnation of the proposal. So, if the King were still determined to marry, he would have to abdicate. He recognized this himself now, and resigned himself to departure.

By this time Mrs Simpson had already left the country in the company of the King's friend, Lord Brownlow, and had gone to stay in Cannes. From Cannes, under Brownlow's guidance, she issued a statement that she was 'willing, if such action would solve the problem, to withdraw from a situation which [had] been rendered both unhappy and intolerable'. It was a well-intentioned, though pointless gesture. Hardinge dismissed it as meaning 'exactly nothing'; the King, when Mrs Simpson read it to him over the telephone, agreed to its publication, but insisted that it didn't make the slightest difference. And, despite the welcome accorded it in the press, where it was interpreted as an ideal formula, it did not, indeed, make any difference. The King was more determined than ever to marry, and, since this now meant renunciation of the throne, he would renounce it.

By Thursday 10 December when this decision became generally known, there had been a noticeable change in the climate of public opinion. Only a week before, the King had been seen as the unfortunate hero of the drama, thwarted by a wily government; but as the issues had become clearer he was cast in an increasingly less flattering role. As Brian Inglis has pointed out in his detailed account of the whole affair, the public's 'first instinct had been to assume that the King, whom they liked, was being got at by his Ministers whom they did not like.... Not until Baldwin's Commons speech [on 4 December] was the nature of the constitutional crisis formally clarified. But as soon as it was, people began to realize that Baldwin had a case.... The King, people felt, was behaving out of character. He had stepped out of his fairy tale: Prince Charming might marry a princess, or he might marry a Cinderella, but he certainly could not marry a Mrs Simpson.'

'Opinion in the country had settled down steadily behind the Government,' Leo Amery confirmed in his diary, 'and the country as a whole was getting progressively more shocked at the idea that the King could hesitate between his duty to them and his affection for a woman.'

Certainly once the King had gone, few sincerely regretted his departure. There was widespread sympathy for him, of course; but there was even more sympathy for his successor who had taken the significant and reassuring title of King George VI.

182 *The Prime Minister, Baldwin, with Edward in an earlier, more carefree year*

183 *(Right) Queen Mary and King Edward visit the Cenotaph on Armistice Day, November 1936*

184 (Left) In America there were no inhibitions about speculating on the King's relationship to Mrs Simpson. A mural on the wall of a California hotel bar put the issue plainly

185 In October Mrs Simpson's divorce came up for hearing in Ipswich. On 26 October the New York Journal positively stated that some eight months after Mrs Simpson's divorce decree was obtained she would be married to Edward VIII of England. The article was said to have been written by press magnate William Randolph Hearst himself (below), who was then staying in England

*186 (Left) Despite his personal worries Edward carried
on his routine programme. Here he is seen inspecting
the crew of H.M.S.* Escapade *at Portland on 13
November*

*187 Edward's last public appearance at the British Legion
Festival in the Albert Hall on Armistice Night*

188–190 By 17 November, when Edward travelled to Wales, the issue between King and Prime Minister was clear: abdication and marriage, or King and no Mrs Simpson. Walter Monckton advised the King, while (189) Sir John Simon advised Mr Baldwin (190)

94 *The formula of a morganatic marriage was put to Baldwin, but soon proved unacceptable. By 1 December the tension broke, and the British press in turn broke silence. Edward sent Mrs Simpson, with her aunt, Mrs Buchanan Merryman, out of the way to Fort Belvedere*

195 *The first week of December in London was
unendurably strained. In Royal Lodge, Windsor
Great Park, there were regular family conferences*

196 (Left) In the meantime Mrs Simpson had fled
from Fort Belvedere to France, where she stayed at
Cannes with her friends, Mr and Mrs Herman
Rogers. Lord Brownlow, who had escorted her from
England, declared to a press conference at the Hotel
Majestic, Cannes, that Mrs Simpson was willing
to withdraw from the situation if such an action
would solve the problem

197 The sympathy of the crowd outside Buckingham
Palace was clear. Insistently they sang 'God Save
the King'

*198 Crowds in Whitehall waited eagerly for news of
fresh developments*

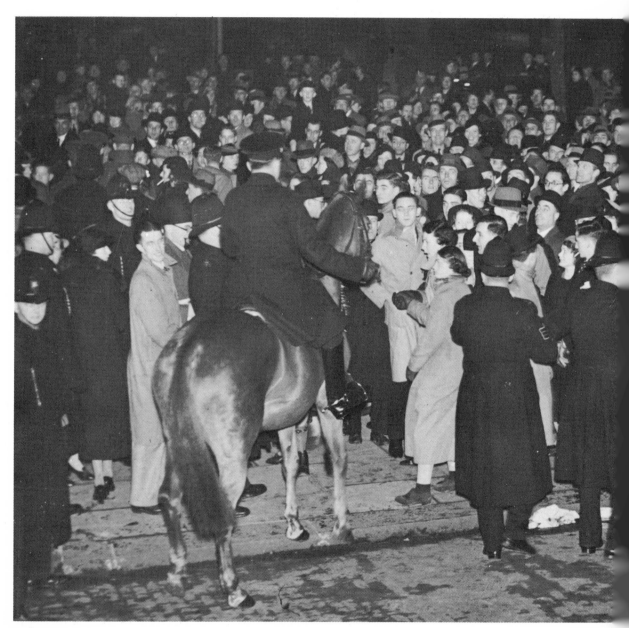

199–203 In Parliament Mr Attlee, Leader of the Opposition (below left), played pat-a-cake with Mr Baldwin at Question Time, whilst the Prime Minister drummed up support from the Empire – from men like Mackenzie King of Canada (below right) and De Valera of Eire (left hand column, opposite), who took advantage of the crisis to prepare fundamental changes in the Irish constitution. On 10 December Mr Baldwin announced in Parliament 'A Message from his Majesty the King signed by his Majesty's own hand'. He handed it to the Speaker, E. A. Fitzroy (top of right-hand column), whose hand trembled whilst he read the message. From the Augusta Tower in Windsor Castle, the gruff voice of Sir John Reith (below, right-hand column) was heard: 'This is Windsor Castle. His Royal Highness, Prince Edward.' The moment of abdication had come

204 On Sunday 13 December, the Archbishop of Canterbury, Cosmo Lang (seen below at a later date), whose attitude to the prospect of a twice-divorced Queen had been crucial throughout, made his broadcast to the nation. 'With characteristic frankness he [Edward] has told us his motive. It was a craving for private happiness. Strange and sad it must be that for such a motive, however strongly it pressed upon his heart, he should have disappointed hopes so high and abandoned a trust so great.'

205 (Right) Flashback to 1919. Edward and Winston Churchill had been friends since the Investiture. Together they had composed the King's farewell speech

206 *Directly the King's broadcast was over, he fled through the night to Portsmouth, where he boarded the destroyer* Fury *and sailed for France*

207 *(Right) On 3 June 1937 Edward married Mrs Wallis Warfield Simpson at the Château de Condé, near Tours*

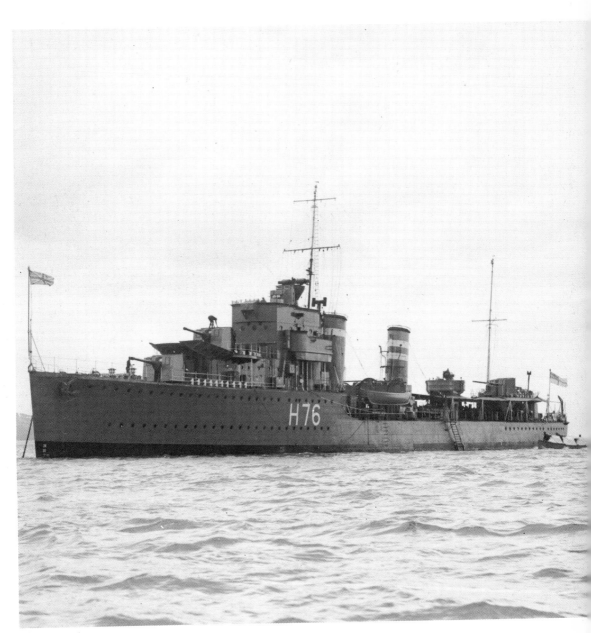

6/Return of a Field-Marshal

'He did not want to give up his baton.'

The Duke and Duchess arrived back in England after nearly two years abroad on 13 September 1939 and went to stay with 'Fruity' Metcalfe at his home in Sussex. The next day the Duke went to see the King and offered his services in 'any capacity'. The King, who had already given some thought to the problem, suggested that his brother could be employed most usefully as a member of the Military Mission to France; but that, if he agreed to this, he would have to relinquish the rank of field-marshal, which as a former sovereign he still retained, and revert to that of major-general for the duration of the war. The Duke said he would think about it.

The more he did think about it, the less the suggestion appealed to him. He had no objection to going to France; but he did not want to give up his field-marshal's baton, and he considered that, before re-embarking for the Continent, he ought to be given the opportunity of making a tour of the various commands in England so that he 'could be in contact with the soldiers again.' With these ideas in mind, the Duke went to the War Office on 15 September to see the War Minister, Hore-Belisha. The call was made unofficially and in secret; the Duke arrived in civilian clothes and hurried through the ministry door carrying a gas-mask.

Hore-Belisha had been at Oxford with the Duke and, as Minister of Transport, had often seen him subsequently during the campaign to reduce road accidents, a campaign in which the Duke had taken a lively interest. After the abdication, Hore-Belisha had been the first British Cabinet Minister to pay an informal call upon the Duke in Paris. They were well disposed to each other, and Hore-Belisha would have liked to have helped the Duke; but as the details of the Duke's proposals were made known to him, Hore-Belisha, so he recorded in his diary, 'began to see difficulties.' The Duke reluctantly abandoned his idea of remaining a field-marshal when it was pointed out to him that to relinquish the rank would be a unique sacrifice; yet he did insist that the Duchess, who wanted their villa in the south of France to be used as a convalescent home for British officers, should accompany him not only in Paris but also on his previous tour of the commands in Britain. Hore-Belisha had not been prepared for this. He had heard that the Duchess wanted to run a hospital on the south coast of England. He feared that the King would not at all like the idea of her touring all over the British Isles in the Duke's company; and his fears were fully justified. The next morning he was summoned by the King who 'seemed very disturbed and walked up and down the room . . . in a distressed state. . . . He said the Duke had never had any discipline in his life. . . . He thought that if the Duchess went to the Commands, she might have a hostile reception, particularly in Scotland. He did not want

208 An historic visit to Berchtesgaden, Hitler's mountain
    retreat, in October 1937

the Duke to go to the Commands in England' at all.

Hore-Belisha, promising that he would try to arrange the matter satisfactorily without bringing the King's name into it, had to leave for a meeting of the War Cabinet before he had managed to allay His Majesty's anxiety. He was pressed to return to Buckingham Palace that afternoon when the meeting of the War Cabinet was over. At half past two, accompanied by Ironside, the Chief of the Imperial General Staff, he returned to the palace where he found the King in as agitated a state as ever, protesting that all his ancestors had succeeded to the throne after their predecessors had died. 'Mine is not only alive', the King complained, 'but very much so.' He reiterated his anxiety about the Duke and Duchess travelling about in England, and asked Hore-Belisha and Ironside to do their best to persuade his brother to go to Paris immediately.

Within half an hour Hore-Belisha was back at the War Office where the Duke was waiting to see him. 'He expressed his pleasure at going to the commands in England and making contact with the soldiers,' Hore-Belisha recorded later. 'I pointed out that when a soldier was given an appointment, he invariably took it up without delay. I explained that the troops were moving about, the secrecy involved, and that the Duke's presence would attract attention. It would create an excellent impression with the public, I said, if the Duke showed readiness to take up his appointment [in Paris] at once. . . . The Duke appreciated all the arguments and expressed agreement. The difficulty, therefore, of his going to the Commands was solved.'

The Duke then asked if his brother, the Duke of Gloucester, was being paid as Chief Liaison Officer with the British Expeditionary Force and added that he himself had come back to offer his services voluntarily, that he did not want any payment, and that he would like this to be announced in the press. He also asked if he could wear his decorations on his battledress, and if 'Fruity' Metcalfe could be appointed his Equerry. Hore-Belisha assured him that everything would be done 'to make things easy and pleasant for him and that his chauffeur would be enlisted as a soldier. . . . The Duke left after about an hour. A small crowd had collected outside the War Office. They gathered round his car and cheered him as he drove away. He seemed very pleased, smiled and raised his hat.'

The Duke's tour of duty in France was shortlived. A few days after the German invasion of the Low Countries, on 15 May 1940, he left for Biarritz, and then, towards the end of the month, he made for La Cröe, his villa in the south. He was at La Cröe while the last British troops were being evacuated from Dunkirk and he was still there when he heard the news of Italy's entry into the war. Nine days later, having made up his mind that he could remain in France no longer, he and the Duchess left for Spain by way of Cannes, Arles and Perpignan. They were accompanied by an English officer, the Duke's personal detective, the Duchess's maid, their chef, and three dogs. The going was slow: the roads were crowded; there were barricades at the entrances to the larger towns and they were repeatedly stopped and required to show their papers; food was difficult to procure and they were glad of the biscuits and tins of sardines that they had prudently taken with them. At Perpignan there were further difficulties and delays. An official at the Spanish consulate declined to grant them a visa, asking, instead, for the Duke's autograph for his grandchild. The Duke said that he would give it in exchange for the visa. But the Spaniard was not tempted by this offer. Finally the Duke managed to persuade him that the fugitives would be vouched for by an old friend, Jose Laquerica, the Spanish Ambassador to France. So at last their passports were stamped and they were allowed across the frontier.

The Duke's arrival in Madrid and the terms he set for his future employment were reported to Berlin where they aroused the deepest interest. The Nazi leaders had long cherished the notion that the Duke and Duchess were sympathetic towards National Socialism and the ambitions of Germany in Europe. It was an ill-founded notion, but there were reasons for its existence. Unlike his father and grandfather the Duke liked Germany and its people. Indeed, before the war his supposedly pro-German feelings created widespread dismay in certain London circles. 'Much gossip about the Prince of Wales's alleged Nazi leanings,' Henry Channon had confided in his diary in June 1934. 'He is alleged to have been influenced by Emerald [Lady Cunard] (who is rather éprise with Herr Ribbentrop) through Mrs Simpson. The Coopers [Duff and Lady Diana] are furious, being fanatically pro-French and anti-German. He has just made an extraordinary speech to the British Legion advocating friendship with Germany; it is only a gesture, but a gesture that may be taken seriously in Germany and elsewhere.'

Certainly the Germans themselves believed that they had an ally at court in Mrs Simpson. When Hitler had appointed Ribbentrop to the German Embassy in London, Goering had objected to so idle, arrogant and incompetent a man filling so important a position. 'The Führer pointed out to me', so Goering later reported, 'that Ribbentrop knew "Lord So and So," and "Minister So and So". To which I replied, "Yes, but the trouble is that *they* know Ribbentrop."' Nevertheless, Ribbentrop did have friends in London; and one of the most influential of them was believed to be Mrs Simpson.

When she and the Duke of Windsor turned up in Madrid in 1940, Ribbentrop was convinced that he could make use of them. According to captured German Foreign Office documents, Ribbentrop was informed by the German ambassador in Madrid, on the authority of the Spanish Foreign Minister, that the Duke had 'expressed himself against Churchill and against this war.' He was 'convinced that if he had remained on the throne war would have been avoided, and he characterized himself as a firm supporter of a peaceful arrangement with Germany.' In the event of his terms for re-employment by the British proving unacceptable, he had decided to settle in Spain in a castle which was to be provided for him by Franco's government.

By the time this information reached Ribbentrop, the Duke had left Madrid for Lisbon where he was making arrangements for his voyage out to the Bahamas. Ribbentrop was determined to do all he could to prevent him. In a 'Very Urgent, Top Secret' telegram, he ordered the German Embassy to do their utmost to induce the Duke and Duchess to return to Spain where they were to 'be persuaded or compelled to remain'. 'At a suitable occasion,' Ribbentrop's telegram continued, 'the Duke must be informed that . . . Germany is determined to force England to peace by every means of power and upon this happening would be prepared to accommodate any desire expressed by the Duke, especially with a view to the assumption of the English throne by the Duke and Duchess. If the Duke should have other plans, but be prepared to co-operate in the establishment of good relations between Germany and England, we would likewise be prepared to assure him and his wife of a subsistence which would permit him . . . to lead a life suitable for a king.' To Walter Schellenberg, a young officer of the SS who was to go out to Portugal and endeavour to bring back the Windsors to Spain, Ribbentrop added that 50 million Swiss francs would be made available to the Duke, and that the Führer was 'quite ready to go to a higher figure'.

The Germans, so their captured documents suggest, now informed the Spanish government of their plans and arranged for an old Spanish friend of the Duke, Miguel Primo de Rivera, to go to Lisbon to invite the Duke to return to Spain for a hunting holiday and for a conference about Anglo-Spanish relations. Believing that he was acting for his government, Rivera did as he was asked. 'He had two long conversations with the Duke,' the German ambassador subsequently reported; 'at the second one the Duchess was present also. The Duke expressed himself very freely. . . . Politically he was more and more distant from the King and the present British government. The Duke and Duchess have less fear of the King, who is quite foolish, than of the shrewd Queen who is intriguing skilfully against the Duke and particularly against the Duchess. . . . When Rivera gave the Duke the advice not to go to the Bahamas, but to return to Spain, since the Duke was likely to be called upon to play an important role in English policy and possibly to ascend the English throne, both the Duke and Duchess gave evidence of astonishment. Both replied that according to the English constitution this would not be possible after the abdication. When Rivera then expressed his expectation that the course of the war might bring about changes even in the English constitution, the Duchess especially became very pensive. . . .'

A few days after this report was despatched to Berlin, Sir Walter Monckton arrived in Lisbon to urge the Windsors to depart for the Bahamas as soon as possible. The Duke seems never to have seriously contemplated any other course once he had satisfied himself that he would not be welcome in England on the terms he had stipulated. Schellenberg did his clumsy best to frighten him and the Duchess into seeking refuge in Spain by having stones thrown at their windows and then circulating 'rumours amongst the servants that the culprits were agents of the British Secret Service' who were reported to have received orders to assassinate him. But, as the German ambassador complained, it was not easy to exert influence on 'the pronounced English mentality of the Duke'. He was not easily frightened; and he had no real interest in the 'prospect of free political activity from Spanish soil'. Indeed, when the German documents were released for publication many years later the Duke maintained that they were 'complete fabrications and, in part, gross distortions of the truth'. He admitted that overtures had been made to him by Nazi sympathisers to return to Spain rather than to take up his post in the Bahamas; but at no time did he 'ever entertain any thought of complying with such a suggestion' which he 'treated with the contempt it deserved.' In a final attempt to deter the Windsors from leaving Lisbon, Schellenberg spread a story that a time bomb had been hidden in the liner *Excalibur* in which they were to sail. The Portuguese held the ship until a thorough search had been made. No bomb was found. Ribbentrop's absurd plan had entirely failed. And the Duke and Duchess sailed out into the Bay of Biscay on 1 August.

209 *The summer of 1938: at Antibes, on a Mediterranean*
    cruise with Mr and Mrs Herman Rogers

210 In September 1937, the Duke and Duchess of
Windsor were in Hungary as guests of Charles
Bedaux, the powerful industrialist who had strong
right-wing views. Edward planned to study labour
relations in America, but his friendship with
Bedaux caused opposition from U.S. labour leaders,
and his visit was cancelled

211 *In early October the Duke and Duchess visited the Paris Exhibition*

212 *(Overleaf) Instead of going to America afterwards they visited Germany – to study labour relations*

213 (Left) In July 1938 the Duke and Duchess were
cruising on the yacht 'Gulzar', owned by a member
of a Greek syndicate at Monte Carlo

214 Autumn 1939, the outbreak of war: the H.M.S.
Kelly, with Lord Mountbatten in command,
raced to Le Havre to bring the Duke and Duchess
back to England. In the background is Major
Randolph Churchill, wearing military uniform

215 On 13 September the Duke and Duchess were staying quietly in a Sussex village

216 (Right) On 18 September Edward, carrying briefcase and gas mask, was cheered at the War Office

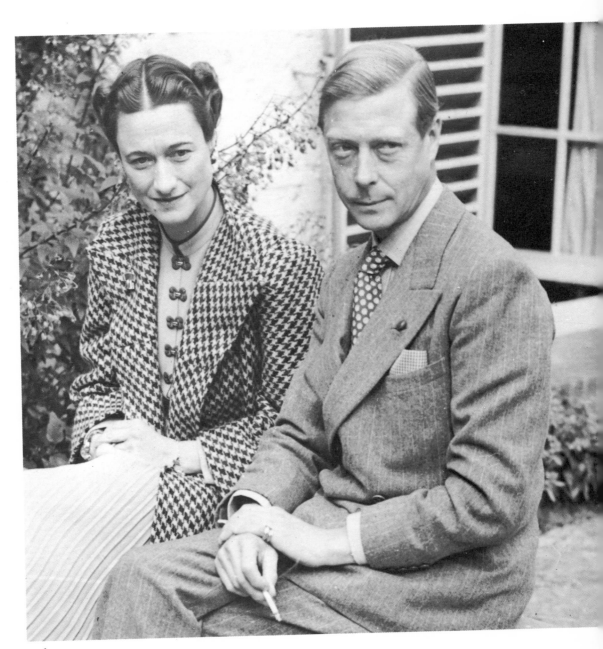

217 December: back in France, with General Lanoix at St Germain-en-Laye

218 (Right) After the fall of France Edward was given the job of governing the Bahamas. On 29 August 1940 he took the oath

219 (Left) In January 1941 Edward flew to meet
    Roosevelt. Here he enters the launch which is to
    take him to his plane

220 In the Bahamas the Duchess was President of the
    Bahamas Red Cross. She shows the Duke some of
    the supplies they were sending back to England

221 *A visit to the United Aircraft Co., Hartford,*
   Connecticut in November 1941. Together he and the
   general manager rode along the final motor assembly

222 *(Right) A visit to the annual Miami air show, 1941*

Celebrating St David's Day at the R.A.F. station at Nassau, in the Bahamas, 1943

226 *Inspecting the R.A.F. camp at Windsor Field, Nassau*

227 *Edward's yacht 'Gemini' at Nassau*

228 *(Left) With the war over, Edward lost his job. He hoped for another and in October 1945 landed at Hendon*

229 *One year later the Duke and Duchess were in England staying at Ednam Lodge, Sunningdale, when they were robbed of the Duchess's jewels – said to be worth £50,000. The Duke shows his solicitor how it was done*

230 In October 1945 Edward met Queen Mary at
Marlborough House for the first time in nine years

7 / Exile

'It was impossible to forget that he had once been King.'

After the war, the matter of his wife's title still not being settled to his satisfaction, the Duke went to live in France, making occasional visits to England for family celebrations and funerals and for shopping. He did not come for his niece's coronation as it would not have been in accordance with constitutional usage, so he declared, for him to attend as a former sovereign. But he was in England for his brother's funeral and for his mother's where he was observed in Westminster Hall 'looking nervous and fidgetty, but obviously very unhappy'.

He was still happy, though, in France. Henry Channon met him there in the summer of 1950 for the first time since the abdication. The Duchess was 'elegant and gay and gracious', Channon recorded. 'The Duke rather desséché, astonished me by his opening remark which was "do you remember the night we dined together at the Saddle and Cycle Club in Chicago?" (This was in 1924 or 1925!) He watched me talking to Wallis; evidently he is still passionately in love. He came up three times and interrupted us by bringing her Scotch and water . . . each time she smilingly accepted the glass, and put it down undrunk. There was certainly understanding and affection in her glance.'

The Duke and Duchess lived in Paris in a large stone house on the edge of the Bois de Boulogne. They also had a country house, the mill at Guf-sur-Yvette, south-west of Paris, where they turned the outbuildings into guest houses and where the Duke created a beautiful garden as he had done at Fort Belvedere. They lived a quiet life, though they were the undisputed leaders of French society, attended numerous functions in aid of charities, and entertained in truly regal style. Their chef was acknowledged to be the best in Paris; their footmen wore the royal livery; they had twenty-one servants in all. As *The Times* correspondent wrote, 'some of his friends have said that it was impossible, however intimate one became with him (and he was the most approachable of men) to forget or be unaware that he had once been King.'

His house, with its family portraits, its standards and banners in the hall, its various mementoes and objects on display, though a friendly and comfortable home, had an unmistakably royal atmosphere. The Duke himself, however, remained quite free from pretension. He still enjoyed dressing up, and still appeared at the dinner table in a variety of evening wear, including Highland dress; he spoke easily to his guests in that faintly American, Long Island accent which he had aquired so many years before; after dinner he would sometimes play gin rummy for low stakes or – one new pleasure, at least, that his self-imposed exile had brought to him – read a book.

In 1964, while in America, he underwent an operation for aneurysm of the abdominal aorta; and the next year, in London, had several operations on his left eye. In February 1972 he had a hernia operation at the American hospital in Paris; and from this operation he never fully recovered. By the early summer he was known to be dying. When the Queen and the Duke of Edinburgh, having gone to France on a State visit, called to see him in May, he could not get downstairs and was obliged to receive his niece in a sitting-room on the first floor. Ten days later, in the bedroom next door, he died.

232 Rumours of a rift refuted with a clinch on board
Queen Elizabeth, *December 1950*

233 *On 7 January 1947 Edward posed with his wife and*
Lord Inverchapel, the British Ambassador (second
from left), in Washington

234 *With occasional exceptions the photographs of the*
Duke and Duchess taken in the post-war years are
predictable – posed portraits. In November 1948 they
attended the first post-war horse show in Paris

235 *Washington, D.C.: letter-writing, 1947*

236 *With Lord Inverchapel in Washington, the same
year*

237 Outside their summer house in Locust Valley, 1948

238 and 239 By 1949 Edward was taking his golf very seriously. He was playing at Deauville with a handicap of fourteen

240 *In Paris the Duchess gives their English butler his orders for the day*

241 *In New York Edward inspects 'Old Faithful', the Humber touring car used by Montgomery in his North African and Italian campaigns, April 1950*

242 *Arrival in New York, December 1949: the Duchess had just been voted the second best-dressed woman of the year*

243 *They had left Paris on 21 December*

244 *Posing with their specially built station wagon at*
Palm Beach, Florida, on 23 March, 1950

245 *At their villa in Biarritz, 1951*

The death of George VI brought Edward back to England, and he walked in the funeral procession on 15 February, 1952

249 *The death of Queen Mary brought Edward to Marlborough House on 25 March, 1953*

250 *In April negotiations were drawing to a close for the sale of Fort Belvedere to King Farouk*

251 *Holidaying in Rome, July 1952*

252 *Leaving Claridge's – to cries of 'Welcome home, Teddy': December 1953*

3–260 (continued overleaf) Shopping in the North End Road, Fulham, in December 1953. By the time that the Duke and Duchess have left the antique shop, a large crowd has gathered outside. As they walk towards their car they express their own surprised pleasure and leave behind a happy and excited group of Londoners

261 November 1956: back in London for the first time since 1953

262 (Right) December 1959: dancing at the Paris Lido

266 *In May 1972 Queen Elizabeth, Prince Philip and
Prince Charles visited the Duke and Duchess during
their State visit to France*

267 *(Right) Ten days later the Duke – aged 77 – was
dead. The sadness hollowed the face of his beloved
wife, glimpsed at the window of her room in
Buckingham Palace where she was staying for the
funeral by invitation of the Queen*

268 *(Overleaf) In the cold light of dawn the hearse bears
the body of the uncrowned king home to Windsor
Castle, past the lonely statue of his great-grandmother.
The crowds have gone*

C2.